NEW BRITISH DESIGN

Rifat Ozbek, living embodiment of the 'return to classicism' in British fashion – but he adds a touch of wit and irony to soften the blow.

NEW BRITISH DESIGN

EDITED BY JOHN THACKARA

Designed by Stuart Jane

COMMENTARIES BY PETER DORMER

With over 120 illustrations, 80 in color

THAMES AND HUDSON

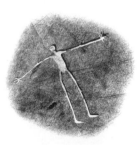

© 1986 Royal College of Art, London

First published in the United States in 1986 by Thames and Hudson Inc., 500 Fifth Avenue, New York, New York 10110

Library of Congress Catalog Card Number 86-50776

Printed and bound in Japan

CONTENTS

THANK YOU

The Publisher and Editor wish to thank Jocelyn Stevens and the Royal College of Art for its most generous support of the research, illustration and editorial work which went into the preparation of NEW BRITISH DESIGN, and for making possible its publication in a popular and accessible format.

We thank, too, Wolff Olins for their great hospitality in extending unlimited studio and administrative support to the project, and for tolerating the disruption which housing a project of this nature necessarily involves.

A third important ingredient in the book's publication has been the generous financial support extended by the following design companies, to whom particular recognition is due for their commitment to the long term development of design talent in the United Kingdom.

Design Marketing Ltd

McColl Ltd

Minale, Tattersfield and Partners Ltd

Alison Cowhum's indefatigable work in assembling and controlling the large quantity of information and illustrations for the book has been superb. Sharon Plant, director of Aspects Gallery, and the Design Council, were most generous with pictures and information. Laura George and Kate Flett were instrumental in compiling the Directory. Shona Wood in organising the picture research.

GREAT BRITAIN has always been a leading innovator and creative force in the fine and applied arts. Just now, British creativity is enjoying a particular renaissance: British architects are winning important commissions around the world; British fashion has been at centre stage for several years; British industrial designers occupy key positions in some of the great design-led companies.

One of the reasons for this success is that Britain is blessed with talent in depth. Our leading designers command wide attention in industry, and in the media; but behind them a confident and energetic avant garde provides much of the creative energy which continues to propel British design onwards.

This new generation operates in a variety of contexts – in our many excellent art and design colleges; in small design consultancies; in a legion of small companies, shops and galleries; on occasion, on the staff of big companies. Their very dispersal has meant that their work has not until now been noticed and appreciated by the public.

It was with some enthusiasm, therefore, that I agreed that the Royal College of Art should be involved in a project to gather the best of Britain's _new_ design together for publication. The Royal College has a long history as one of the major crucibles of art and design development in Britain, and it is consistent with our ambition to enhance Britain's design profile on a broad front that we should help publicise this new generation.

An exciting feature of the book is the multi-disciplinary character of the work which the research uncovered. It can only increase our confidence in the future that designers and artists are, variously, collaborating together, organising their own display and production, and engaging constructively with industry in the search of quality and innovation upon which all our futures depend.

Jocelyn Stevens
Rector
Royal College of Art

James Dyson: his G-Force vacuum cleaner is a talisman for the redesign of traditional products.

INTRODUCTION

British avant garde design today is a vivid expression of the tensions that affect us all in the modern world. On the one hand there is the rapid modernisation of technology and industry, with all that implies – automation and flexible manufacturing, new materials, systems, software based 'adaptive' products, and so on. On the other hand there is modernism, our cultural and aesthetic response to the implications of all this progress – unemployment, de-skilling of work, the feeling that technology is out of control, fear of impending nuclear catastrophe or war.*

The formal argument for design has been articulated with skill and conviction in recent years, but the reality today is that design continues to be regarded as a technical, problem solving activity by industry, and by consumers as an ephemeral, cosmetic attribute of a small range of products. Design's potential as a process which synthesizes the benefits of technology with the aspirations of its users remains unfulfilled.

British design will no longer sell as a novelty item; it will come to be judged on the basis of its performance in solving some of the key problems of the day: innovation, and the perpetual changes in technology; the changing needs of consumers around the world; the revolution in production, and saving human skills; challenging the received wisdoms of design itself.

The value of the avant garde is that it challenges the critical atrophy which has allowed this marginalisation of design to persist. This is not to suggest that designers of strange, impractical, and certainly uneconomic artefacts are 'better' than their professional colleagues working productively with industry. On the contrary, we need both. Mainstream design can only benefit from pressure from below that it broaden its horizons.

*See Marshall Berman's 'All That is Solid Melts Into Air'

In this context, one thing is certain: 'classicism', per se, does not, despite recent suggestions to the contrary, have the answers to these unique, contemporary problems. It becomes clear, when you ask people what they mean by classicism, that they refer not to some Platonic, problem-solving technique based on truth and purity, but to something more mundane: a clean and tidy lifestyle, filled with simple but beautiful things, that is not polluted by the mess, uncertainty and discomfort of the world at large. There is nothing unworthy about this range of aspirations —it's just that classical design by itself won't meet it. The only exception is if you are rich enough to insulate yourself against the influence of offices, traffic systems, information processors, robots, nuclear weapons and the like – in which case you probably own a private, de-bugged space shuttle in which to escape.

So although fashionable people may well dress for a while in Chanel dresses and classic suits, the rest of design is going to have to press onwards in the belief, shared by most of the designers represented here, that design is no longer just about *things*. In an increasingly synthetic and de-natured world, there is a need, first, for products which are more sympathetic to our emotional and sensual needs. And second, as software and systems spread to all areas of life, design must also start to grapple with intangible phenomena and not confine itself to products made in factories which you can touch and feel.

This is quite a challenge, because design has been stereo-typed as a much more limited activity during recent years, particularly in Britain. Dating back to Mrs Thatcher's 'design seminar' at No 10 Downing Street in 1982, the period saw government spending on design promotion triple from £4 million to £12 million a year, and the involvement of design consultancies in the revamping of high street shops throughout the country. The successful launch of several large design groups on the Stock Exchange was further proof that design had become a significant service industry. The trouble was that 'design' began increasing to be used as a marketing prefix in its own right; although design is a process, it was transformed by marketing – speak into a commodity. As the hype increased, consumers quite rightly began to ask whether design was really *this* big a deal.

The fundamental problem for older, industrialised countries such as Britain and the USA is that they face a 'hollowing out' of their manufacturing base, a process which, ironically, involves a high design input. More and more 'domestic' products contain imported technology with a high added value, the home-side's contribution being to assemble and package them. Many 'British' cars, 'British' computers and 'British' consumer durables are nothing of the sort. The graphics, styling, instrumentation and packaging may be carried out by designers, but the economically more important research and development is done overseas.

There is talk now of a 'technological plateau' in the West, a generalised resistance to more and more innovation for its own sake. A majority of designers seem to be unaware of this groundswell of opinion, in part because so many remain utopian believers in the idea that technology is necessarily a good thing on its own account. This is why so many architects still dream of ordered, sanitised environments, free of mess and human debris; the controlled solution, the technological fix, remains attractive to a generation of designers educated in the modernist tradition. An uncritical relationship with technology also helps explain the continued use of 'high tech' imagery in products and environments, despite clear signals that consumers are looking for more sensuous, softer, 'natural' qualities in their surroundings. It's the Jaguar versus BMW syndrome. The Jaguar's 'soft' technology and craft-rich interiors are incredibly attractive to consumers who don't wish to feel they are riding around in a spacecraft. But these particularly English design qualities are missing from most British industrial design, which has cut itself off from a tradition of hand-made artefacts.

The irony is that while mainstream design remains uncritical of technology as an idea, it has also failed to meet the challenge posed by the revolution in production techniques. Any awareness of such marvels as automation, or flexible manufacturing systems, is usually confined to the expectation that they offer another way of reducing costs. Less attention is given to the functional and affective qualities that the new technology can provide – for example, greater product differentiation, or 'hand-made by robot' craft finishes.

In industry this leads to the systematic undermining of the contribution of human skill and labour to the production process. Voluble talk about 'design for ease of manufacture' has disguised a progressive collapse of industry's skill base. In common with management strategy generally, too much of today's design is informed by the belief that capital and machines are more important than people, a division of labour between thinking and doing that is reinforced by professional self-interest – the 'keeping the experts expert' syndrome.

This is not meant to imply that contemporary design is to *blame* for the continued decline of manufacturing. Management itself, in most companies, helps sustain the outdated demarcation lines between production, design and engineering; only a minority of companies have started seriously to retrain craftsmen as operators of complex systems, for example too many skilled workers are stranded tending obsolescent machines. *Everyone* resists the full-scale flexibility that new technology makes possible, but designers, who are uniquely well placed to change things, to act as catalysts at the centre, have yet to exploit this opportunity.

This somewhat gloomy balance sheet of the state of design in industry today can, thankfully, be qualified by two more hopeful trends, both of which are documented in this book.

The first is a new and more constructive engagement between industrial designers and a new breed of enlightened manufacturers. Rather than act as technicians, asked to revamp old products, or to package imported technology, some designers have been asked to come up with long-term, 'blue sky' product ideas, or even, perish the foreign-sounding thought, 'concepts'. Freed of the requirement to design products to suit existing production lines, their job is to look at new technologies and materials, and at new consumer needs, and ask 'why not?...' rather than 'can we?...'

But it would be foolish to suggest that these early experiments have been painless. On the one hand, not all designers are articulate, and sometimes fail to get their ideas, good or bad, across. On the other hand, the management of design remains an undeveloped skill in industry, to put it mildly. Innovative design projects usually only succeed when there is an 'enabler', or product champion, at the top of the hierarchy – someone who supports the designer's challenge to existing practice.

Other designers have given up hope of finding sympathetic partners in industry, and are exploring ways of manufacturing and distributing their own products. To some of this group the Italian experience is an inspiration; that country's success in furniture, lighting and clothing has been due, in part, to the survival of a lively artisan tradition, based in a small-scale workshop infrastructure, which makes it possible to produce, in small batches, products which could not economically be made in huge factories. The problem is that Britain's industrial base is not Italy's. In common with the USA, Britain has more vast and outdated production complexes than small workshops. Many British clothing and furniture designers, for example, have despaired of finding suppliers at home who are capable of meeting the quality and reliability standards necessary to compete in world markets; they have ended up sourcing their production overseas. In some industries, such as textiles, this trend is being reversed, and designer-entrepreneurs are once again manufacturing in Britain. But the majority still find it increasingly hard to get their products made. James Dyson's G-Force vacuum cleaner, a talisman for product designers trying to revamp traditional products, is a typical example; after years of effort it is now made in Japan.

The relative lack of influence wielded by design in manufacturing stands in contrast to the much greater impact it has had on the consumer in recent years. Shops have been improved, and a whole range of services, from travel and entertainment, to finance and advertising, have been transformed. The trouble is that the quality of our experience in highly designed hypermarkets, high-tech interiors, 'theme pubs' and starter homes, is not demonstrably superior to life in *less* designed locations. On the contrary, the prefix 'designer' has become, in some cases, a byword for unsympathetic, artificial and over-controlled environments, or a marketing device used to sell poorly conceived, over-priced goods. We should also note that in the structure and composition of the profession, and in much of the work carried out, mainstream design tends to reinforce male stereotypes and a tunnel-visioned interpretation of the 'man-made' world. This is why many women, as consumers or as designers, have been less ecstatic about the design boom than their male colleagues.

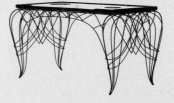

The design of today's thoroughly modern consumer, service and leisure enterprises *is* technically proficient, but it can also be manipulative, and aesthetically bankrupt. In fact the very *word* 'aesthetic' has become anathema to market or production-led design.

The systematic exclusion of aesthetic and sensuous delight from much of today's product design is the reason why we have included so much 'craft' here. As my colleague Peter Dormer notes in his commentary (page 99), the value of Britain's much-noted craft revival itself tends to be over-rated. Of the 20,000 plus craftspeople active in Britain, few are very good. But among a minority, there is much innovative and exciting work, both in terms of ideas and of production quality.

The fact that most of these individuals are alienated from mainstream manufacturing is a tragedy, for it means that their work is only available, in small expensive quantities, to a minority. If even a few of their innovations in form, or surface finish, or materials handling, could be taken up by manufacturers, dramatic improvements to mass production standards could be made. Imagine a washing machine with its bland steel panels made more interesting by the metal finishing techniques developed by craft jewellers; think of furniture with the qualities of a 'one-off', produced in quantity; even car interiors could be improved by the use of more original textile designs.

Although some craft designers work in the 'rustic idyll' tradition which horrifies many industrial designers, the majority of those included in this book use advanced materials and contemporary imagery. Jane Dillon's wardrobe, for example, is 'hand-made', but it is made of space-age aluminium sheeting; Tom Dixon's 'salvage' furniture is made by hand, but it incorporates industrially made bits and pieces, and is sensitive to the possibilities of mechanism.

A corollary of craft's renewed significance is the emergence of crossover between previously discreet design disciplines. The very word discipline is harshly appropriate in a culture such as our own which frowns on attempts to blur distinctions. A high degree of professional self-interest is vested in their maintenance. When architects start designing clothes, or painters underground stations, or jewellers hats, *bad* architects, painters and jewellers get nervous.

This is not to argue that crossover, or multi-disciplinary design, is good for its own sake, as was said of multi-media art and performance during the seventies; the benefits of crossover are more practical than ideological. But breaking down barriers has *become* politically charged because the economic interests of the specialists are perceived to be threatened.

The avant garde in Britain may almost be defined by reference to its rejection of obsolete creative boundaries. Painters, particularly those operating outside the gallery system, are more likely than graphic designers to have the inclination, let alone the time, to challenge prevailing imagery and visual technique. Sculptors, unlike most product designers, are *supposed* to experiment with the tactile values of materials and the geometrical qualities of new forms. It is the *job* of performers to create drama and to involve the audience, whereas design tends, if unwillingly, to be isolated from the people it affects.

But what really matters is not this or that artist dabbling in 'applied' projects, or the small number of individuals experimenting in new media. The 'opening to art' in design is significant because it represents the first signs that the super-rationalistic, anti-nature, mechanistic world view of planners and designers is beginning to soften.

One medium through which the connection between art and design is made, albeit a contingent one, is fashion, where sensuality and awareness of the 'spirit of the times' combine. Another is environmental design, where the so-called 'soft' factors, such as heat, light, texture and colour, have become just as important as 'the plan' — but require a different sensibility on the part of the designer. It's a case of more Matisse than Mies.

There is a danger, however, in an obsession with sensuous gratification by itself. As Edward Timms has observed, 'aesthetic delight ultimately dissolves into existential anxiety', a dilemma widely represented here. For every designer absorbing the sensuous potential, and the techniques, of craft, there is another addressing, in theoretical terms, the *technological* context, and the awareness that *nothing stays the same*. Anything containing software, from individual products to whole factories, has ceased to have a fixed function — and it can be unsettling.

The American artist Robert Irwin has talked about the artificial barriers 'which keep art from dealing with the universal experience of change'. The same goes for design. Irwin's response has been to create environmental works for public spaces that encourage the viewer, as user of the space, to look around with the eye of an artist.

No finite work of art can compare in importance, for Irwin, with this individual act of perception. In this he is echoing the point made by Marcel Duchamp, who observed that the artist performs only one part of the creative act; the other part is up to the onlooker, whose response, or interaction complete the creative cycle.

Some of the designers in this book pay direct homage to these ideas. Daniel Weil, for example, who researches the forms appropriate for today's technology, considers the *user's* experience of his 'objects' to be part of the design process. His work questions the form of products whose functional components are minute or, in the case of software, invisible, adding an aesthetic dimension to the 'functional' arrangement of the hardware.

The so-called 'salvage' design too, a good deal of which is shown here, reflects in its attitude to the design of cities and streets where most of us live, our general apprehension that things are not working as smoothly as surface appearances suggest. For example, the work of NATO ('Narrative Architecture Today'), recalls a quotation in Thomas Berger's 'Crazy in Berlin' in which an ex-GI wanders around the war-blasted city asking 'why, when things are broken, do they seem like so much more than when they are together?'. There is something much more human-scaled about a lean-to shelter, or about the bits and pieces of junk that make our surroundings familiar. NATO questions the artificiality of inflexibly planned cities, mass-produced artefacts, in fact all the dehumanised patterns of life in the 'man-made' world. Trash and junk are invoked as a powerful antidote to the over-rational design of cities and objects.

It is in their critique of pure rationality that the significance of designers like Nato, Daniel Weil and others lies: they are the performers of leaps in imagination that the planners, the MBAs and accountants with their tables of numbers, are unable to make. There will always be a need, of course, for designers who can manage the whole of a product, or idea's development from conception through to production; but not *all* design needs to be based on this model. In software, for example, much design work already proceeds in an incremental, jerky, hands-on manner. The same goes for the ever more complex human-technical systems, such as power stations,

communications networks and the like: it is literally impossible for a designer to work out in advance, by application of reason, how the finished result will look. Systems design has to be interactive, absorbing the unpredictable responses of people, or machines, as it progresses. This is not necessarily to suggest that plants like Three Mile Island should be run by artists! – rather, that treating them like ordinary machines is to court disaster.

All this talk of design as a service, a kind of 'knowledge consultancy', rather than a technique for making specific objects, may strike some readers as a somewhat exaggerated extrapolation from the work we have collected in this book. After all, there is not much software, no control rooms, relatively little high technology at all; there *is* a wide variety of artefacts, some of which are novel in appearance, others familiar. The point is that we have attempted in this book to capture the spirit of the period through the places and objects of designers who are only now beginning their careers – designers who tend to be critical of current design and manufacturing organisation. Few of them are anti-technology or anti-industry. If we can set up a dialogue between a few more designers, producers and consumers, then the exercise will have been worthwhile.

The book is not intended to be a definitive, comprehensive directory of every new designer working in Britain. Think of it rather as a snapshot, taken in a crowded room: it contains atmosphere, people, movement, but not everyone present is in the viewfinder. That said, some categories of design *are* notably under represented. Graphic design is an obvious example: British graphics are among the technically most proficient, and sometimes wittiest, in the world, but despite extensive research we found little that was startlingly *new*; we suspect we took our snapshot during a brief breathing space in a sector which can be expected to surprise us all again soon. In textile design, too, we were disappointed to find so modest an amount of serious innovative work in an usually buoyant field. We anticipate further editions of this first volume, when these disparities may have evened out.

John Thackara

13

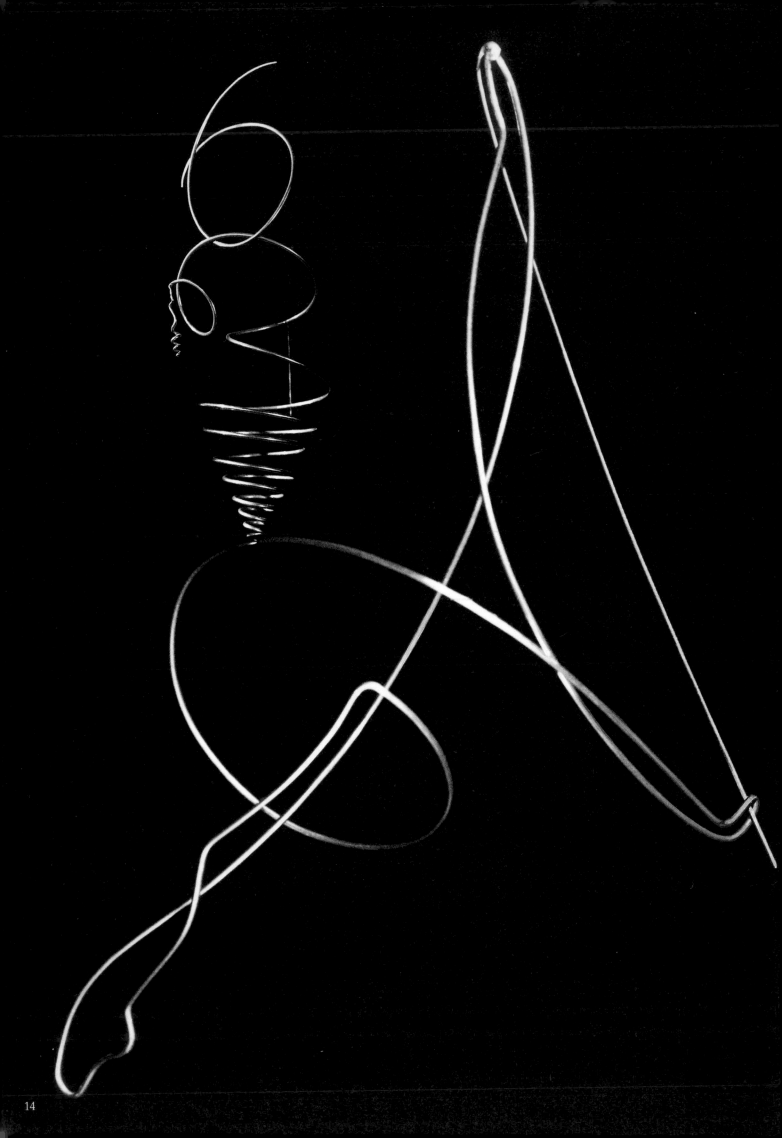

NEW FORMS

Many jewellers do custom 'accessorising' for clothing designers' biannual shows
which provides context and feedback that can be missing from secluded workshops.
Tom Binns *Left* broaches commissioned by Rifat Ozbek *Photography Calum Colvin.*
Judy Blame *Above* crowns for John Galliano *Photography Mark Le Bon.*

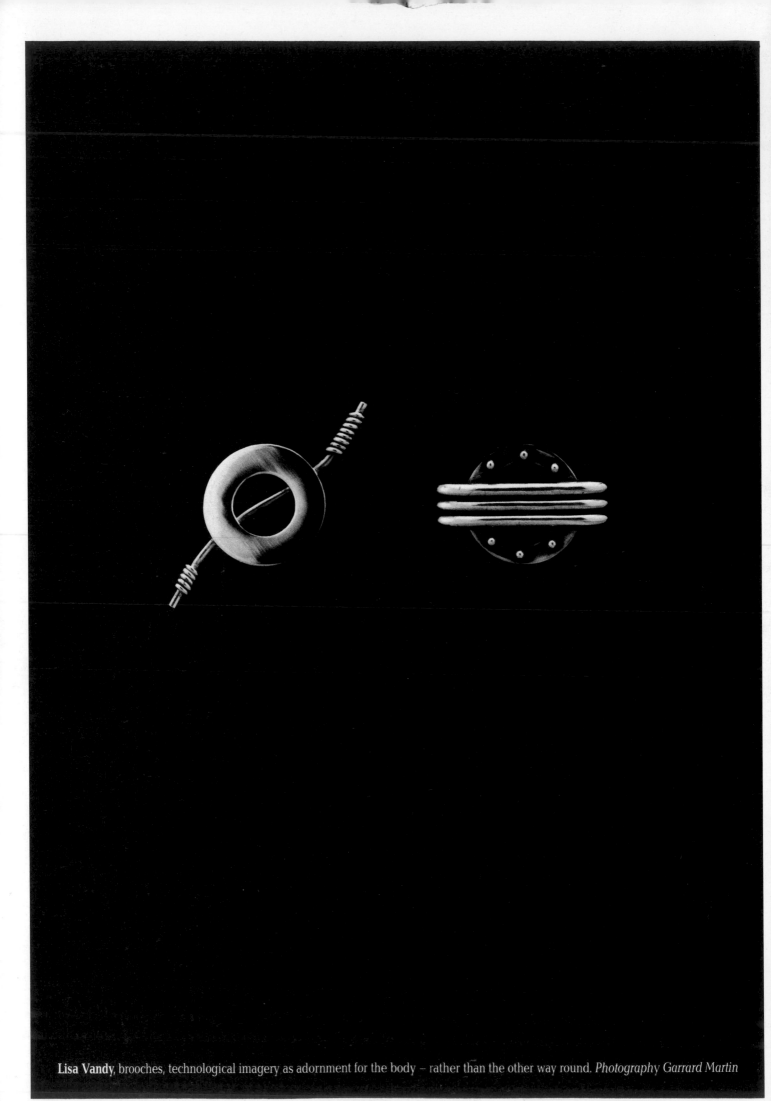

Lisa Vandy, brooches, technological imagery as adornment for the body – rather than the other way round. *Photography Garrard Martin*

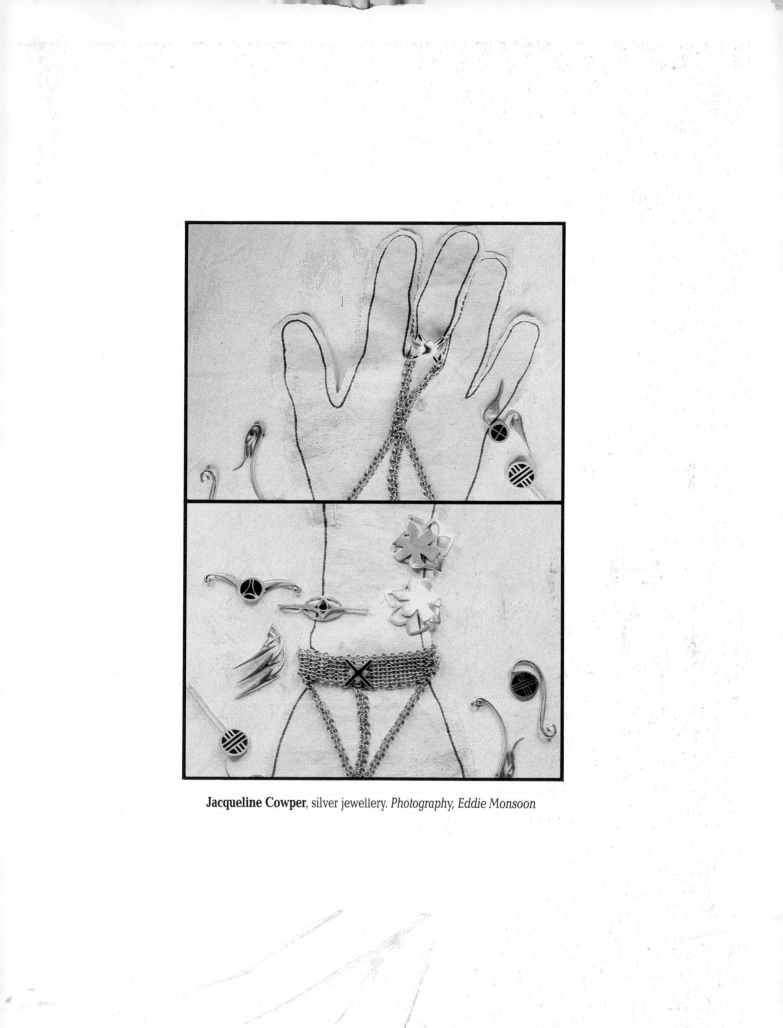

Jacqueline Cowper, silver jewellery. *Photography, Eddie Monsoon*

Maura Heslop,
etched steel brooches.
Photography, Garrard Martin

David Watkins, 'Voyager', neckpiece in 5 parts, neoprene coating on wood and steel

Sasha Ward, painted glass panel. The use of glass to enhance the effects of daylight indoors was widespread in Northern Europe until the Twentieth Century. Now, glass is making a comeback

Hand-blown glass *(inset)* by **Tim Shaw**

Architectural stained glass
by **Alexander Beleschenko**

Oriel Harwood, ceramic horns *(below)*, a proposal that the primeval swamp is one alternative source of imagery to the junk-yard

Nicole Hood, hand-painted, factory produced plates, *(above)*
'slapping the industrially designed product around the face'

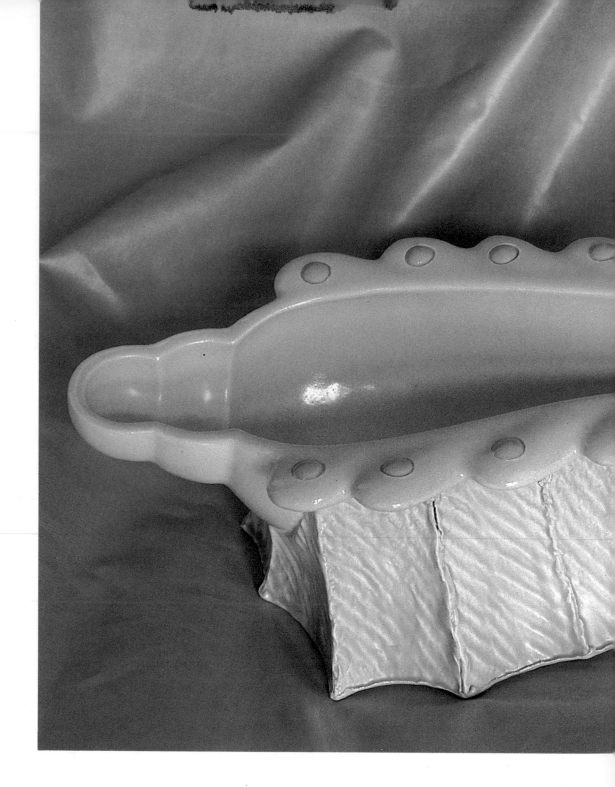

Richard Slee,
ceramic dish.
Slee is a master
of the ironic
historical reference;
and of surrealist
surface finish

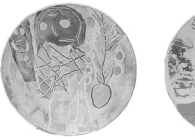

Susan Nemeth,
press-moulded, slab-built
porcelain bowls

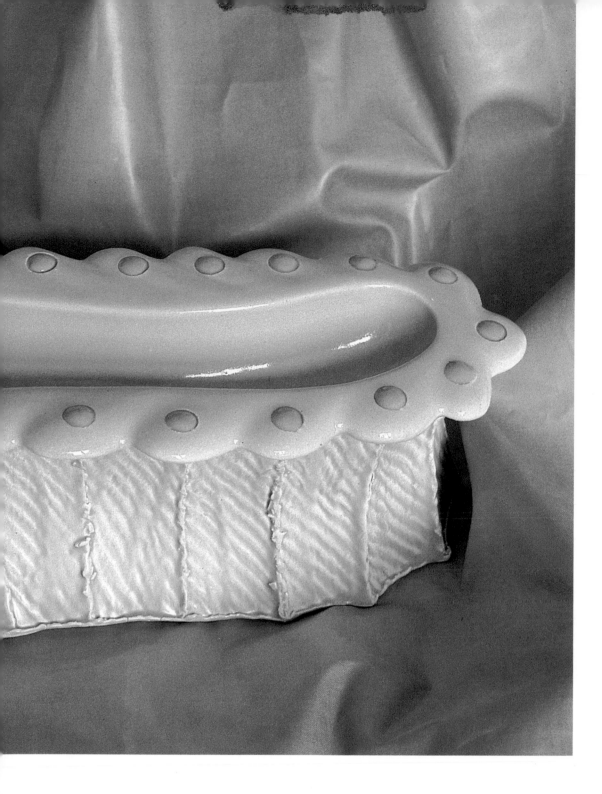

Esperanza Romero,
architectural ceramics.
A generation of architects
is re-learning the use
of hand-made building details

Marion MacDonald earthenware and terracotta pots. *Photography Garrard Martin*

Jenny Amon 'Sea Cucumber' *(left).*
Jorge Luis Borges meets The Third Man.
Photography, Calum Colvin

Douglas Barber, model for motorcycle,
with unique front fork configuration
Photography Alex McNeil

Matthew Archer, prototype miniature computer. The pouch is leather and contains the segmented components for the miniature computer; the white discs store the information; the dagger-like instrument is a single-handed keyboard

Paul Priestman, domestic radiators, sculptural replacements for objects whose ugliness is legendary

Seymour/Powell, motorised bicycle developed for General Electric Plastics. The 35cc two stroke engine and petrol tank is integrated with the wheel

Atlantic Design (Ros Appleby), 'Atlantic Dryer', chrome hairdryer for men. A fine mixture of Brunel and 1930's cruise liner aesthetic

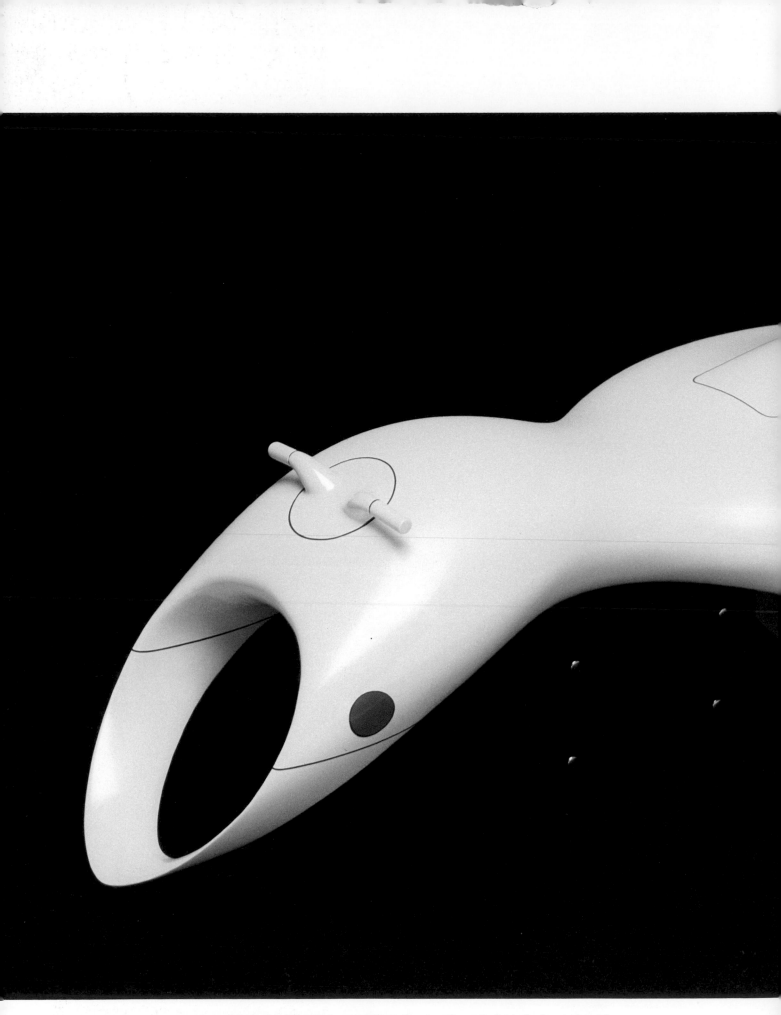

David Cole, prototype personal hydrofoil. Waterborne sculpture, the aquatic equivalent of a fun motorcycle

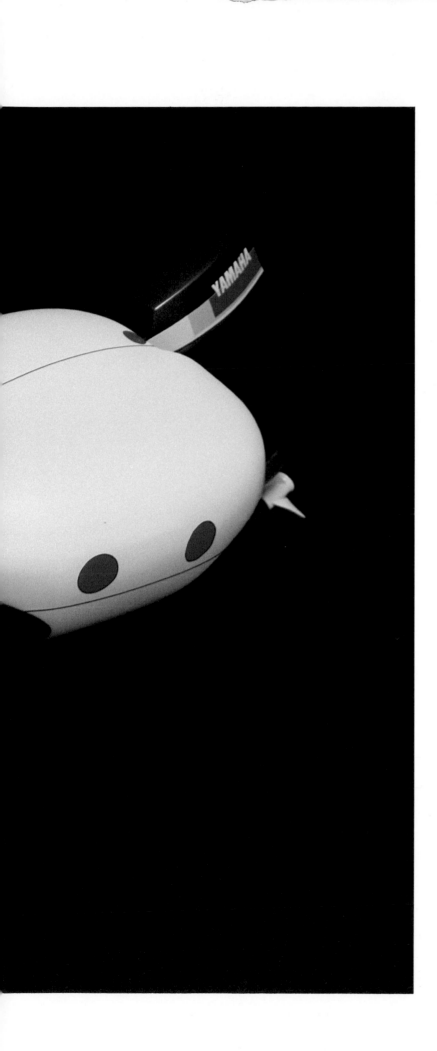

Random Design, 'Synthaxe' *(top),* a key piece of recent British high technology industrial design, a balanced and effective combination of mechanical and electromechanical components. Designer Ian Dampney supervises electronics packaging from prototype, through testing, to production, using computer aids to control much of the process. **Geoff Hollington,** computer chess set *(above),* made in Hong Kong – where the power of design to add value to electronic products is appreciated more keenly than in Europe. **Chris Barlow,** prototype cassette player *(below).* A graduate of the Royal College of Art, London, Barlow applies sculptural wit to hitherto dull consumer products

Andrew McRae, colander and jug with mugs,
a more elegant and composed re-working of common domestic artefacts
than 'designer teapots' and similar mannered attempts of recent years

Gary Morga, ''Hephaistos' (main picture), mesh and arrow lamp

Gary Morga, 'Aphrodite', bent aluminium lamp. A product which can be made with the simplest of equipment

Paul Priestman, megaphone. You can speak and look at the audience at the same time. *This award-winning design has been put into production by the Japanese*

Chris Barlow, 'Kneeling man television': the medium is the Messiah

Paul Atkinson, micro light clock *(left)*, steel, brass and optic fibre – with an added dash of sunlight, and hieroglyphics of indeterminate origin

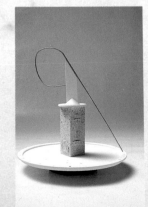

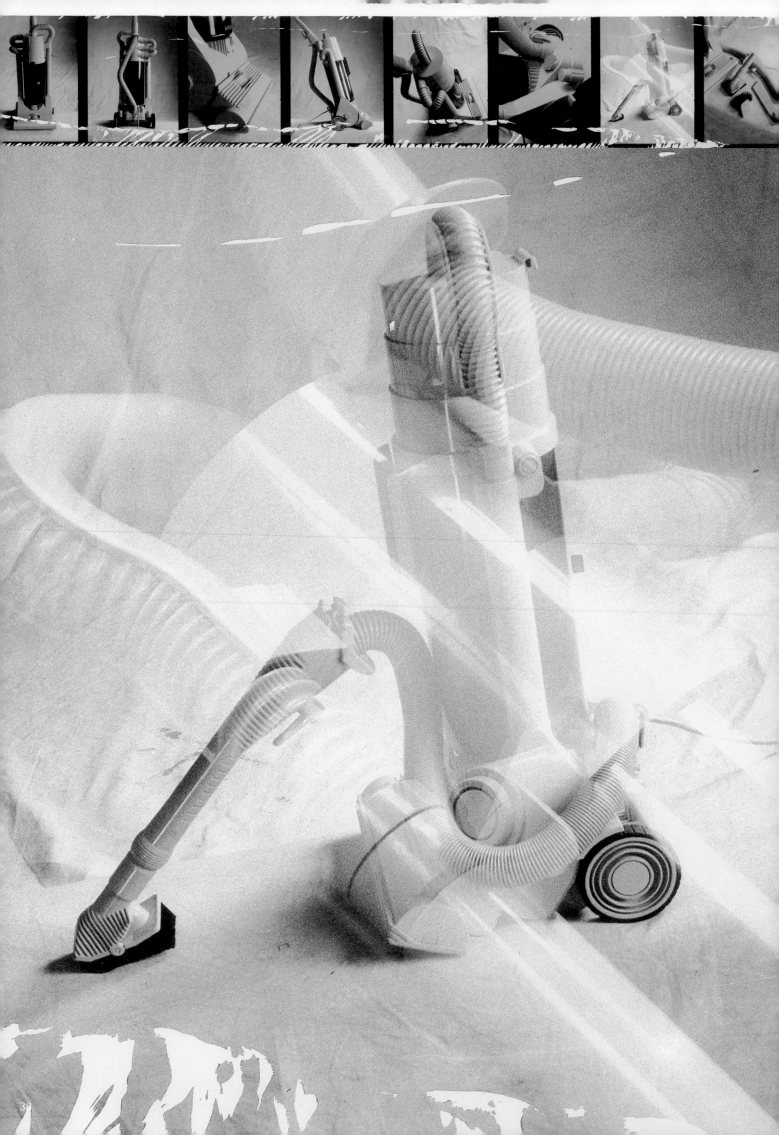

Daniel Weil, three band radio *(above)* – NASA meets the English country house **James Dyson,** 'G Force' cyclonic vacuum cleaner *(left)*. This is a radical redesign internally and externally. Dyson is an example of a breed of British design entrepreneur who is not content to let a good idea be ignored for, despite the usual indifference of British manufacturers, he has managed to get this into production – by the Japanese

Daniel Weil, 'clock', etched copper, steel cutlery, electronic components, wine glasses, transformer and micro chip. The circuit board is no longer miniaturized, and any quantity of cutlery can be used to link the transformer to the board

Ron Arad's 'One Off' gallery and shop in London has acted as a focus for austerity-chic in design, or as he puts it, *'design and art, new and old, accidental and incidental.'* Shown here: 'Horns' aluminium chair. *Photography, David Buckland*

Paul Huxley (*left*) interior mosaic for Kings Cross Underground Station, Piccadilly Line, London. What distinguished this scheme from other artist-led refurbishments are the colour relationships – Huxley, an abstractionist, understands colour.

Tag Design (Tony Wills and Greg Hole), models of screens for use in the Lloyds of London Headquarters designed by architect Richard Rogers. A touch of softness in this citadel of mechanisms

Nigel Coates (Branson, Coates, Architects). Metropol Restaurant, Tokyo, Far-Eastern flagship of Anglo-Gothic chic

Tom Mitchell researches perceptually based design from the academic perspective of psychology and art. He is attempting to predict how environmental changes affect people psychologically or perceptually – 'environment' being taken to include ambient music and sound, light intensity, colour and image complexity, and these factors in combination.

NATO (Narrative Architecture Today), Gamma City exhibition at the Air Gallery, London

David Hiscock, untitled photographs

Hiscock took sculpture by Gina Martin to create sculptural environments *Photographs courtesy of Vogue*

Filmic influences (above, and opposite): Derek Jarman's Caravaggio; furniture by **Daniel Grey**

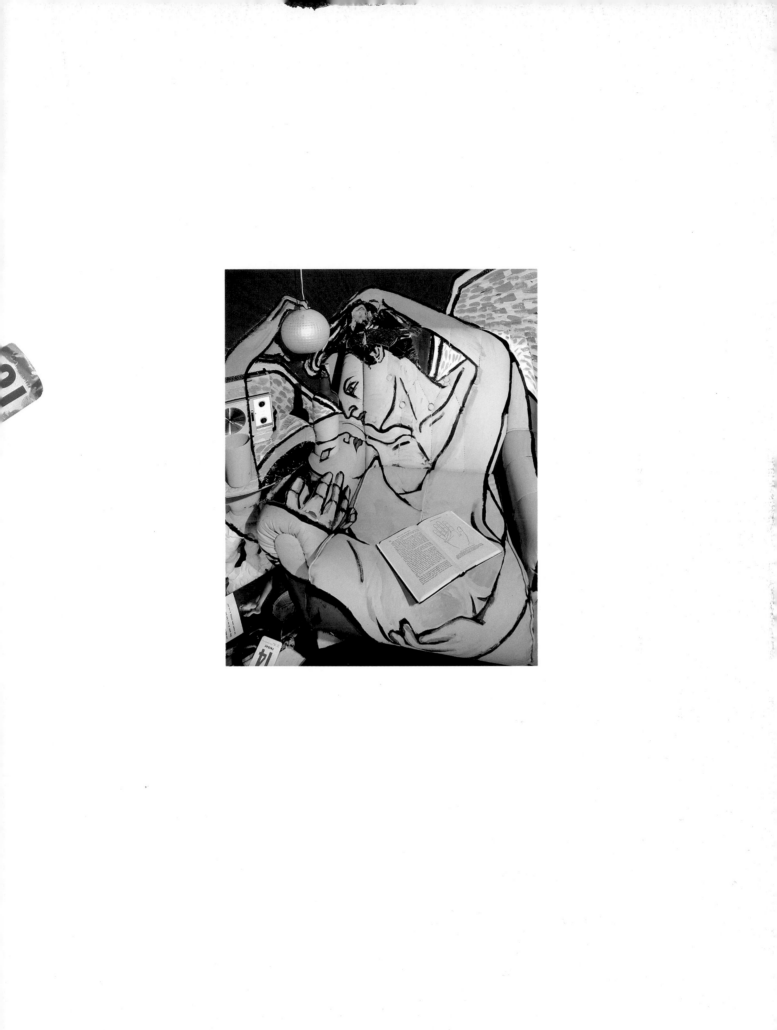

Calum Colvin, 'Death of Venus' *(left)* and 'Cupid and Psyche' *(above)*, installations

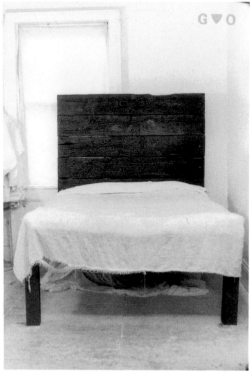

Daniel Grey furniture: *(top left)* dovetailed joint construction chair; *(below left)* large dining table incorporating railway sleepers, finished in molten iron; *(above)* high-rise bed with branded headboard; *(below)* The Grey Organization

Daniel Lane, detail of glass screen *(background)* and table *(inset)*. Daniel Lane has exploited furniture to pull in decorative art and sculpture

Daniel Lane, glass table

Tom Dixon, chairs. Dixon, like André Dubreuil, gives the chair spirit and makes it dance – reclaiming it from the moralising attitude of the Bauhaus 'fitness for purpose', or worse, the tendentious 'We know best for you' authority of Utility furniture

André Dubreuil, table (left) and chairs (right and overleaf): his work combines the acerbity of salvage with the romance and posture of the Cavalier

Jim Horrobin, *(left)*
one of a new generation
of designer blacksmiths

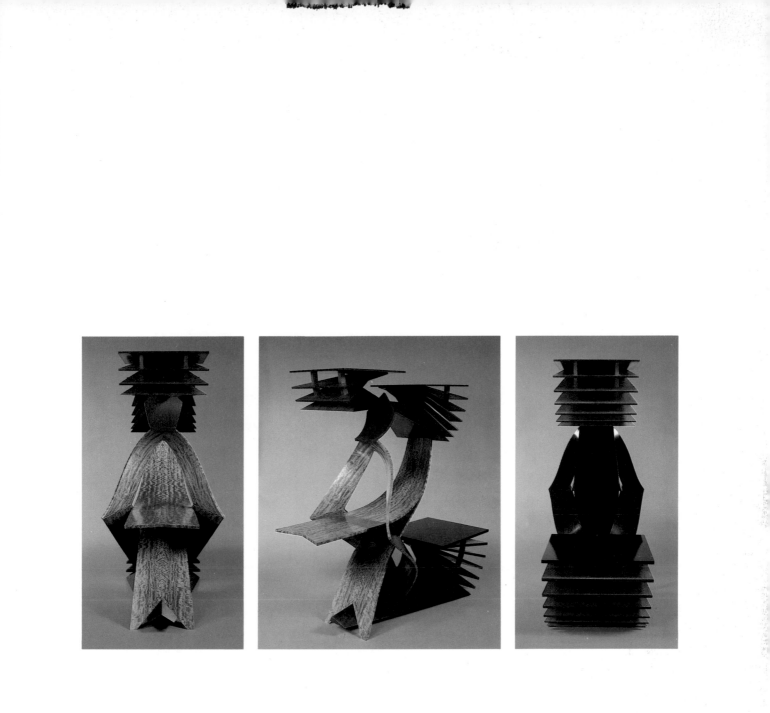

Fred Baier, 'Megatron', veneered plywood. Baier has taken modernism for a walk through the 'thirties. He pokes fun in a good humoured way at a time when the trend is to be sardonic

Jane Dillon and Julian Gibb, (*top*) two wardrobes made from honeycombed aluminium (doors), steel, wood and silk – a soft-tech fantasy inspired by childhood memories of these mysterious, huge, household objects. **Mary Little,** chair, (*above*) probably the most accomplished example produced in Britain for five years.

Fric and Frack, (*top left*) domestic table lights made from salvaged material. This kind of expressive, metaphorical design is made possible by the relaxation of attitudes towards figuration. **Lisa Vandy,** (*top right*) sheet metal clock, a sensuous approach to a classic design preoccupation. **Jasper Morrison,** 'Wingnut chair' (*above*) — hardboard and wing nuts. The logic for this extraordinary chair comes from folded paper (look at the back of an envelope).

VISUAL INFORMATION

Dirk van Doren, two expressions of the English mood today. Wax and tissue paper, heavily varnished drawing *(above)* and one of a series of illustrations for an audio-visual presentation *(right)*

Karen Caldicott, 'Jabba Syndrone' (above) 'Avenue B NY NY 10003' (top right) and 'Course of Events' (right)

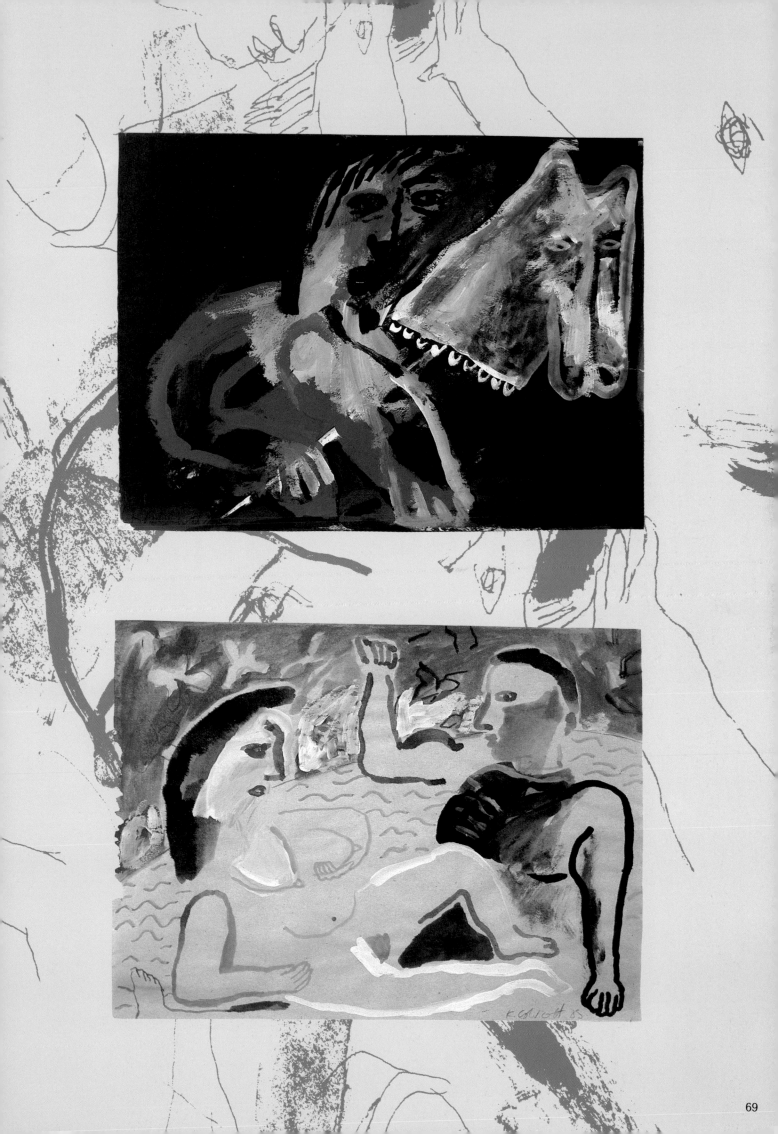

David Blamey, 'Cycling in Holland' (above) 'Towards Ozlem' Izmir Turkey (top right) and 'Amphitheatre' Kas Turkey (right). Blamey occupies that shifting ground common to illustration, graphics and textile design that allows him to work to a variety of commissions

9 - 85   IZMIR

10 · 85   KAS

John England: computer generated image for RCA illustration publicity (unpublished)

Panel 1 (black)

The BAUHAUS mi
stook legibility for c
ommunication, (it's
a man's world).

Nicolette Gray: in n 1 p.12 'It is not really necessary for the beholder to read, or understand these words. THE WORDS ARE PART OF THE MEDIUM ; what the artist is communicating through the medium is his reaction to, his understanding of these words, which he h as expressed in the way they are inscribed.

Six sheets, as if fragments, (keys to a la rger argument/point of view: wider te rms of reference lead to a better, more fully human typography), in order:-

Richard Hunt: in 2 p. 202 'The system was basically very simple. T he stationer h eld a copy of the book (exe mplar) unbou nd in quires o r pieces (peci e), and hired i t out to a scri be piece by pi ece to copy.'

1,2,3,4:

LEFT   RIGHT

FORGET   REMEMBER

SIGHT   SOUND

PRINT   MANUSCRIPT

INTO THE HOT...

James S utton an d Alan B artram: i n 3 p.26 'The Aldine Ro man is the arche type of all Old Face types whic h during the six teenth century e stablished their ascendancy ove r gothic throug hout Europe.'

'Grotesques , which are cl oser in some ways to the b lack letter t han the nor mal roman.'

John Le wis in 4 p.46

Panel 2: LEFT / RIGHT

LEFT   RIGHT

mporarily maki ng it into a kind of skeleton; an d only later do they gradually re-assemble its parts.'

as hair on the head. **Man is matt er & spirit, both real & BOTH G OOD,** & the funny is certainly part of the good. The human body is i n fact a good joke - let us take it s o.'

'Who made me? God made me.'

'The artist gr asps reality i n its entirety a s a complet e, living and i ndivisible en tity.'

U.N.E.S. C.O. Co urier: in n 11 p.74

13 q.1
Mark Br own: in 11 p.60

Oppenh eimer in 11 p.96

'The two halves of the brain are practically physically symmetrical, d ifferent functions or specialisations are found in each one:

(Male
Right hand
Speech, verbal
Logical, mathe matical
Linear, detailed
Sequential
Controlled

'These two ways of **thinking, t** he way of time and history, are both part of **man's effort to c omprehend the world** in which h e lives. Neither is comprehended in the other nor reducible to it, ea ch supplementing the other, **neit** her telling the whole story.'

Female
Left hand)
Spatial, musical
Holistic

Artistic
Simultaneous
Emotional

A. Watts in 11 p.1 29

Intellectual
Worldly
Active
Analytical
Reading, writin g, naming

'The key to the relationship bet ween **yang and yin** is called hsiang sheng, **mutual arising or inseparability,** as Lao-tzu puts it: When everyone knows beauty as beautiful, there is already ugliness

Intuitive
Spiritual
Receptive
Gestalt
Facial recogniti on

Paraphr ased fro m: in 11p.1 31

We are left then, firmly if unknowingly, enslaved to a view of ourselves i SEQUENTIA ; **when everyone knows good** SIMULTANE L n which we are DIVORCED INTO TWO. I am on the one hand M OUS Y MIND AND on the other MY BODY; SPIRIT and FLESH; EG Perception of si **vil.** To be and not to be arise mut Perception of a O and ID. And since as well as the duality I AM ALSO ONE PERSON gnificant order ually; **difficult and easy** are mut bstract patterns ,THE TWO OPPOSITES HAVE GOT TO FIT TOGETHER IN SO Complex mot ually realised; **long and short** are Recognition o ME SORT OF RELATION. Once I assume the division between mi or sequences mutually contrasted; **high and lo** f complex figu nd and matter, spirit and flesh, ego and id, then OF NECESSITY w are mutually posited; **before a** res MIND, SPIRIT, EGO, CONTROL; AND MATTER, FLESH, ID **nd after** are in mutual sequence. ,ARE CONTROLLED.

Ivan Illic h: in 14 p.12

'In fact the vision of new possibilites requires only the recogn ition that **scientific discoveries can be used** in at least tw

Panel 3: FORGET / REMEMBER

FORGET   REMEMBER

Plato: in 16 p.25

In the writings of Augustine we come across a view of language which accords more with everyday experience. Augu 'And in this ins ith the unsatisfa stine put three components together - WORDS, as used in sentences: OBJECTS; and the AIMS of a particular dialogue tance, you who ctory transcienc - and he arrived at a view in which language has a purpose. WORDS ARE SEEN AS INSTRUMENTS FOR ACCOMPLISHI are the father o c of speech, WR NG HUMAN COMMUNICATIONAL OBJECTIVES; instead of being labels. WORDS ARE TOOLS. Against a dominance of f LETTERS, f ITING IS A R surrogation ism. (words as surrogates for ideas or objects), instrumentalism became the basis of much of our educatio rom a paternal ELATIVELY nal system. Grammar is not an end product but a means whereby we can adequately EXPRESS OUR NEEDS AND THOU ove of your ow PERMANEN GHTS. we use words to MAKE OTHERS UNDERSTAND. The dictionary developed in the 16th and 17th centuries, initiall n children, have T FORM OF E y as a means of putting modern languages on a par with Latin and Greek. It began by offering an extensive coverage but been led to attr XPRESSION. I soon assumed COMPLETE COVERAGE - IT WAS A CLOSED SYSTEM. Words became separated from their meanings an ibute to them a 'A LOVE OF LETTERS IS THE d had PHYSICAL IDENTITIES OF THEIR OWN. quality which BEGINNING OF TYPOGRAPHI they cannot ha CAL WISDOM. That is, a love of l ve; for this dis etters as literature and a love of lette covery of your rs as physical entities, having abstra s will CREAT ct beauty of their own, apart from t E FORGETF he ideas they may express or the em ULNESS in th otions they may evoke.' e learners' soul T CAN OVER s, because they COME THE L will trust the ex IMITATIONS ternal written c OF TIME, PL haracters and n ACE, AND M ot remember of EMORY WHI themselves. Th CH INHEREN e specific you h TLY BESET T ave discovered i HE SPOKEN s an aid not to WORD. It is co memory but to mparatively con reminiscence, a text-free, less tie nd you give to y d to the particu our disciples no lar circumstanc t truth but only es of its produc A SEMBLAN tion. WITHO CE OF THE UT THE ADV TRUTH; they ANTAGES C will be hearers o ONFERRED B f many things a Y WRITING I nd have learned N THE CONV

'Syntax: arr angement o f the army (

John Ca ge: in 17 p.11

spects in whi ch **speech** mi ght be **held t** o take prece Norman Bro **dence over w** wn). Languag e free of synt far been disti ax: **demilitar** nguished. Firs **ization of la** es Joyce- ne **nguage.** Jam w words, old syntax. Ancie nt Chinese? **F ull words: w ords free of specific fun ction.** Noun i s verbs is adje ctive, is adver b. **What can be done wit h the englis h language? Use it as ma terial.** Materi al of five kind s: **letters, syl ables, phras**

'your stutteri**N**g's a basket it all**O**ws you to gathe**R** together **More ideAs thaN** a sentence **O**rdinarily woul d be able to hold.' st, as far as is known, **all hu man commu nities had a s poken langu age before th ey had, if eve r they had, a c orresponding written lang uage.** Second ly, every norm

John Ca ge: in 17 p.128

Panel 4: SIGHT / SOUND

SIGHT   SOUND

10,000 M aniscs: n n 19

'any modern man can see, SCIENCE, is TRUTH FOR LIFE, watch RELIGION fall obsolete, SCIENCE, will be TRUTH FOR LIFE,

'The primacy of the wor d carried over into Ch ristianity the belief that all truth and realness, with th e exception of a small queer margin at the very top, **can b**

George Steiner: in 6 p.32

George Steiner: in 6 p.17

'A philosophy of language would return with radical wonder to the fact t TECHNOLOGY AS NATURE, hat language is the defining mystery of man, that in it, his identity and SCIENCE, **of language. It is during the seventeenth ce** historical presence are uniquely explicit. It is language that severs man fr TRUTH FOR **ntury that significant areas of** 'The style is a om the deterministic signal codes, from the silences that inhabit the great LIFE, **truth, reality and action reced** mosaic. Each er part of our being. If silence were again to come to a ruined civilisatio IN FORTRAN e from the sphere of verbal st word is set up n, it would be a two-fold silence, desperate with the remembrance of the TONGUE TH **atement. Between** these langu in its precise word.'

e housed within the walls

George Steiner: in 6 p.30

E ANSWER.' ages **(algebra, architecture) an** and luminou **d** that of **common usage, between the mathe** s place. Touc matical symbol and the w h by touch, Durrell builds his ord, the bridges grow mor array of **sensuous, rare expr** e and more tenuous, until essions into patterns of ima at last they are down...Th gery and tactile suggestion is is a fact of tremendous im so subtle and convoluted tha plication. **It has divided the** t the act of reading becomes **experience and perceptio** one of **total sensual appreh n of reality into separate d** ension. Paragraphs live to th **omains.'** e touch of the reader's hand;

George Steiner: in 6 p.33

George Steiner: in 6 p.45 Eric Gill: in 20 p.5

'THE INSTRU MENT IN OU R HANDS IS WORN BY L ONG USAGE,

'We shall shortly have a s ituation wherein all jokes & eccentricities are the w ork of DESIGNERS- & ma chine-made jokes reprod And the deman uced by the million TEND TO BE BORING' 'IT BECOMES EASIER b

'The style of p olitics and FA CTUAL com munication ve rges on the illi terate. Whethe r in its adverti sements, its co mic books, or its television, our culture liv es by the pictu

they have a **complex aural m usic;** and the light seems to p lay across the surface of the **words in bright tracery.** No one else writing in English to day has quite the same com mitment to **the light and mu sic of language.'**

George Steiner: in 6 p.31

Ivan Illic h: in 21 p. 125

'Only he who '...in choosi discovers **the** ng his text, th **help of writ** e artist cho **ten words** in oses words

Nicolett e Gray: i n 1 p.13

Dental hygiene will never be the same again: promotional brochure for Wisdom toothbrushes

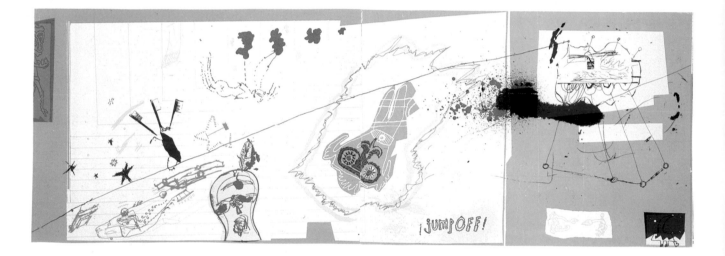

by **Danny Inwards, Tim Hopgood, Robert Ellis** and **John England,** RCA illustration department

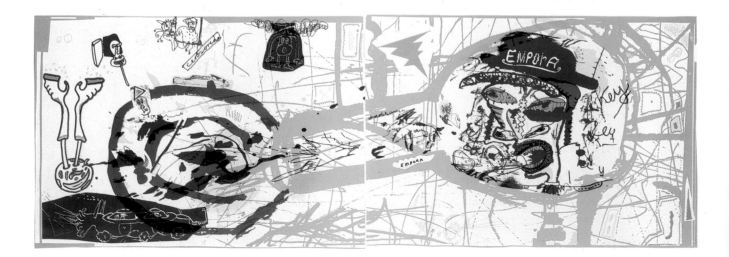

THE BODY

Leigh Bowery, innovative and influential amongst his peers, yet inaccessible in public. *Photography Cindy Palmano*

Georgina Godley: one of the pioneers of Anglo, the new English look of the early eighties. Above and facing page, hand-tailored knitwear for Corgi. *Photography and styling, Cindy Palmano*

Georgina Godley, Couture evening dress, moulded undergarment and elaborate panelled bodice. Photograph, Cindy Palmano

John Moore, 'Tip off', Bump boot with extended sole concept: *'hint, whisper, aside; broad hint, signal, nod, wink, nudge, kick.'*

Richmond Cornejo
(John Richmond and Maria Cornejo)
Autumn/Winter Collection 1986.
Photography by Mark Mattock;
Post-production 'mash' by Eddie Monsoon

Richmond Cornejo, Autumn/Winter 1986. Shoes by John Moore. Photography Cindy Palmano

John Galliano:
(this page and overleaf)
a unique and innovative figure
in British fashion design.
Autumn/Winter Collection 1986.
Crowns by Judy Blame;
Shoes by Patrick Cox.
Photography by Mark Mattock;
Post-production 'mash' by Eddie Monsoon

Judy Blame is probably the leading exponent of 'total fashion' in Britain – he does everything from accessory design and styling, to promotion and communications. It's hard to over-estimate Blame's influence, (although he has been known to do so himself). Christopher Nemeth, salvageer and one-time post-sack thief, is Blame's *'silent partner'*. Both work individually, but the mainstay of their work is as a pair – Blame accessorising Nemeth's clothes, and vice-versa

1 **Christopher Nemeth:** *Early one-off jacket*
2 **Judy Blame:** *'Stolen Property*
3 **Christopher Nemeth:** *Post-sack collection*
Photography: Mark Le Bon

Christopher Nemeth and Judy Blame:
Ancient Briton collection
Photograph by Mark Le Bon

Richard Torry knitwear

Styling by Andra

Photography by Sheila Rock

Kirsten Woodward

Gold Spiral hat *(left)*
dress *by Sarah Windsor*
Leopard Print hat *(right)*
jacket *by Ninivah Khomo*
Jewellery *by Detail*
Makeup *by Jalle Bakke*
Stylist *Finbar, Max Presents*
Photography *Sheila Rock*

Lindsay Keir, hand-painted silk scarves. *Montage Stuart Jane*

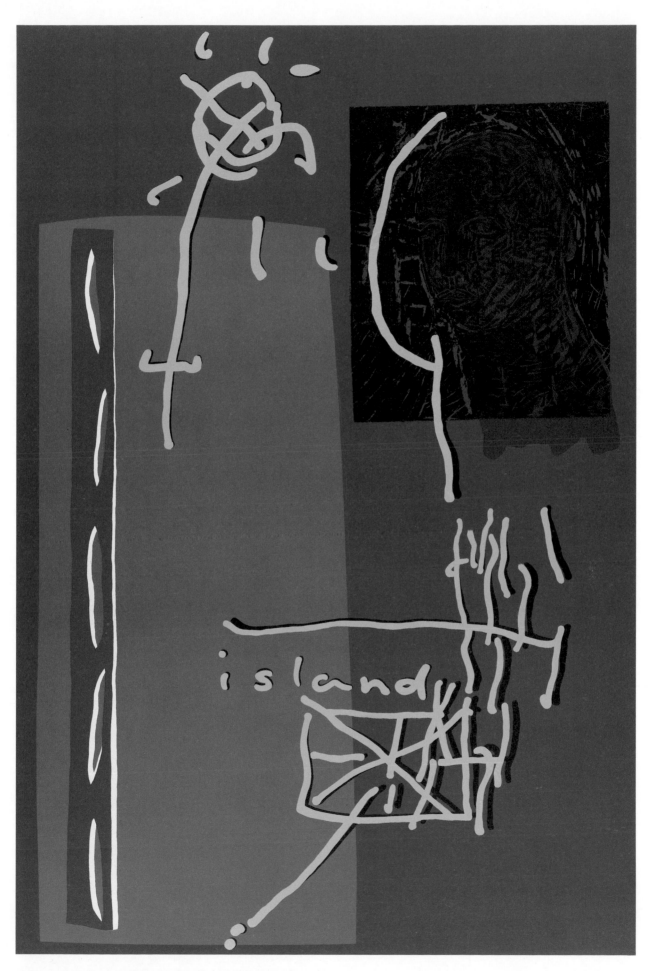

Remo Avella and Paul Burgess, textile. An illustration of the power graphic techniques have acquired in fabric design, where crossover between disciplines is now widespread

Printed fabric by Georgina von Etzdorf

Textile designs by Vonnie Roudette

The Cloth
(Fraser Taylor, Brian Bolger, David Band, and Helen Manning). This studio of four artists produces very strong graphic prints for textiles, some of which are supplied to other fashion designers. Each operates as a painter/illustrator as well as a designer or applied artist
Photography David Hiscock

Wire Up And Finish Painting:
Edinburgh-based design partnership
active in lighting, furniture, textiles,
installations, artwork, books

COMMENTARY

The shopping mall is now for most West European and North American cities what the cathedral was to medieval Europe: a repository of values. This is not necessarily good but it is a contemporary fact. Public attitudes to design in Britain are confusing: there is an intense public demand for conservative values in areas such as furniture, but in fashion, packaging and advertising people expect and even want radicalism and spontaneity.

The British government believes design can revitalise British industry and exports: but with what sort of design should Britain compete? There is a strong market for overtly British goods such as Burberry coats, or Church shoes, and provided no-one becomes complacent there is no reason why the demand for such designs produced to a very high standard should not continue.

But it is pointless to reproduce current designs exported from West Germany, France, Italy or Japan unless such nations are undercut on price and quality. Unlikely. The appropriate strategy may be to leap over today – and tomorrow – and capture the market with *new* design. The Japanese, recognising how they too may be undercut by South Korea and Taiwan, seem willing to treat design as fashion-orientated in electronics and cars. Japan's market is taking to the idea that products can be traded in every year and that different people want many different variations of consumer products. The Japanese are also widening the consumer market all the time with electronic knick-knacks. The morality of this is doubtful: an invent, make and throwaway approach threatens the environment. But at the moment no society knows how to satisfy itself except through economic and material expansion.

A question emerges: is the way forward a constant supply of new design ideas such that design really *is* like the fashion market, one in which last season's radios, hi-fi, cars are definitely out? Or should a nation like Britain seek to assert and then support its own new aesthetic, a new 'British look'? In this book the former is more easily spotted – but in any case there is no "should" or "ought" about it. Things will develop, or not, haphazardly.

This business of 'national' aesthetics is confusing. There is undeniably an Italian or a French look and yet, such is the internationalism of the design world, one is just as likely to turn up a 'foreigner' where one expects a native. One could happily write up about the special qualities of West German car design as exemplified by Audi in happy ignorance of the fact that the head of Audi styling is English.

Things become even more confused when I start claiming Daniel Weil as a British designer when he is, in reality, an Argentinian architect, a former member of the Italian design group Memphis as well as being a graduate of London's Royal College of Art.

But Weil is a puzzle intellectually as well as geographically. Traditionalists among product designers do not know where he fits in, and have tried to shunt him off into the applied arts. Not so. He is an industrial designer. Daniel Weil's work, which looks odd, different, temporary, and disposable, probably shows the way forward.

Perhaps Weil's work appears more strange than it really is because product design is a young (twentieth-century) profession which has ossified too quickly. It went from childhood to a thrombosis-led middle-age without a healthy period of rebellious enquiry in between. Consumer design has been, especially in West Germany, Britain and North America, a conservative contemporary mass medium of visual expression. Weil has challenged the conservatism by introducing design to twentieth-century art. Twentieth-century art in its heyday (shall we say up to the beginning of the last world war) was interesting wherever it made a commentary on the world – and since the twentieth-century artist was relatively free (he had few responsibilities towards clients or patrons) his or her commentary was usually uncensored. Very often the commentary was 'poetic' – you cannot put into words what the art means but you are aware that it means something. Design on the other · hand has always been shackled to clients anxious about 'mass' markets and 'average' tastes. Weil is attempting to shift the attitude towards minority markets and individual tastes – and at the same time use his design as a vehicle for commentary.

For example, Weil has asked why a radio should always be contained in a streamlined box. As he knows there are very good reasons for making radios like simple boxes. People seem to like them that way, they are much easier to produce in mass production, they are easy to package and display, and no-one has to think very hard about how the guts of the radio are put together inside the box. But, in fact, some of Weil's radios, such as those he has placed in plastic bags, are easy to manufacture, display and package; they also happen to be flexible, they can be draped over chairs, hung up on coat racks, or run up flag poles. They also look different, they are a change, they are like a new delicacy for a tired palate.

But it is of radios such as Small Door or the vast clock composed of cutlery (see pages 39-40) that people are prompted to ask, "What is it?" Weil has made something ordered and organised, but which plays at looking chaotic. Small Door looks undomestic, and yet it is given an ultra-domestic floral-patterned cover for the loudspeaker. Small Door is a friendly object (as it should be since a radio is a homely, pleasant thing) yet it is also subversive: it is something of a barbed joke. Why? When manufacturers and design consultants get together they often talk about 'product identity'. That is they want their product to look just that bit different enough for you to notice and buy it (but not too different in case you reject it). Weil's radio takes product identity to its logical illogical extreme.

Weil has not fallen into the trap of relying on the handmade artefact. If he had done so he would have removed his work from the debate about product design. Instead he always uses industrially produced components. His Small Door or his Clock can be made by the thousands and made efficiently. He has not retreated into the isolationism of craft technology.

Breaking the rules happens more frequently these days in furniture design. However, whereas mainstream furniture in Scandinavia, Italy, and West Germany is quite lively, when we look at Britain we see that invention takes place only on the fringe. It is difficult to say how much of this new 'fringe' design impetus is owed to the Memphis group of Milan. Certainly there is some indebtedness to Memphis but there has also been a cross-grained bloody-mindedness present in the field of design craft in Britain for some years.

Quite often when mention is made of the Memphis group someone will quote Britain's Fred Baier (see page 63) as a Memphis rival. This is wrong. Fred Baier's work did not come out of the intellectual interests that characterised Memphis. Baier does, however, illustrate the point that a separate search for new ideas was going on in Britain and is going on in parallel and in some independence of what has happened in Italy. What, however, marks out British furniture and product design in the new 'fringe' is the development of an intellectual attitude. It also puts new British work on a par for discussion comparable with rivals in Europe.

On the fringes of mainstream design (this book's province) and in the broader arena of applied art (also this book's province) literary attitudes, and an inclination towards the theatrical, have come to the fore. Much art and some applied art is completed by words. Thus David Watkins extraordinarily graphic neckpiece (see page 20) is given sense by the title 'Voyager' – a title which completes, confirms or even provides the technological, space age, space travel aspect to the work's imagery. Real life in Britain for many people soon folds into fiction – this must also be true of North America – the land of the television soap opera. Two of Britain's popular newspapers, with a combined readership of 8 millions, serve up as front page news the activities of characters in television soap operas – not, it must be stressed the activities of the actors behind the characters but the characters themselves.

A literary and theatrical attitude marks the architecture of the NATO group – Narrative Architecture Today. I sometimes wonder whether people who live in the West's old, large cities tolerate the quite appalling visual messes that they do tolerate because they each live in a mentally enclosed, fictional world of their own – helped by submerging their ears under the mufflers of the ubiquitous Sony Walkman and its clones. The evocative, lovely crazy illustrations provided by Nigel Coates of NATO in his would-be scrap-metal, post-industrial, judge-as-you-find architecture exist as fictions. Even if anyone attempted to make them they would not be half as poetic in real life as they are on paper. NATO is providing fictional architecture which suggests nostalgia for VE Day (Victory in Europe) – devastated cities dressed with bunting celebrating the end of the war in Europe. It provides a clue to an aspect of current British taste that is echoed in Daniel Weil or emerges in the furniture of Daniel Lane and Ron Arad, and is represented in much of current British painting – a taste for *romantic chaos*.

Romantic chaos always offers the possibility that something good will emerge whilst actually providing an excuse for current failure. As far as Britain in particular is concerned it is a telling point that the one area where British design excels commercially is graphics and advertising – the presentation of two-dimensional fictions. Britons are good at activities such as politics, diplomacy, advertising and packaging: British graphic design is above all else intelligent even at its most blatantly commercial. Graphic design, especially in retail, packaging or advertising is about presenting simple ideas that translate quickly into simple words. But there are also some mainstream product designers who understand the relationships between words and imagery and how this connection adds up to sales. This is where product design is also packaging and where to understand packaging is to understand the diplomacy of design.

The design partnership of Seymour/Powell understands the diplomacy of design. Indeed, although the assumption is that much design is aimed at flattering 'housewives' (with all the attendant assumptions that they are more susceptible to flattery than streetwise men) a lot of flattery is directed at men – the entire electronics, automobile, and defence industries take design cues from the egos of potential male purchasers.

The language of design is considerable. The redoubtable Victor Papanek with his design for the 'real' world which suggested cheap radios made from old bean cans and decorated with beads for the third world was way off course. No one, no matter how poor they are, wants design that speaks patronisingly to them. Seymour/ Powell realise this as can be seen in their motorized bicycle wheel which emerged from a design programme undertaken for General Electric Plastics (see page 31).

The motorized wheel is aimed at existing bicycle owners; the main market potential is in the third world. The bicycle owner removes his or her existing front wheel and replaces it with the motorized wheel in which is integrated a 35 cc two stroke engine and the petrol tank. This motorized wheel can also be used to power other things including waterpumps, flexible drives and generators. It is this flexibility and suitability for low cost one-person businesses or farmers which makes the device economically attractive. Seymour/Powell have devised a modern product without recourse to the 'ethnic' look some Western designers think is appropriate when designing for the third world. The product is easy to assemble, service and maintain – all of which is important given that it is intended to be a reliable, working tool.

One reason why there has been a growth in the number of small design businesses such as Seymour/Powell is partly to do with wishful thinking. It is part of the new realism, the Friedman-Reagan-Thatcher-led street credi-

bility game, to be independent and work for yourself. In any case the successful industries in Britain are often organized as a lot of small companies rather than conglomerates – a fact of industrial life which distinguishes Britain from West Germany and gives her a point of contact with Italy. Fashion is an example. Thus whilst the fashion business is big business economically, it is composed, like the pop music business, of many independent individuals or small firms – each working hard, doing their own thing and making it pay. There's no business like your own business. Secondly, there's no business like show business. The British like dressing up. Amateur theatre thrives, the Establishment still puts on an excellent ceremonial occasion, and generations of Britain's youth have amazed, surprised and even terrified their parents with one radical mode of dress after another.

Most of the interesting design work occurs on the fringe, and it is here that people feel unfetered by over rigid categories. The Cloth, for example, (see page 97) a group of four young designers, operate successfully in fashion, graphics and fine art, bridging different categories. Apart from a lot of work designing textiles for the fashion industry, they have done illustration, record sleeves, interiors and window displays for clients in the pop music and retail industries. Their style is radical, energetic and edgy – it projects that sophisticated roughness fashionable in Britain and which itself stems from a new wave in Britain of expressive painting and sculpture with its roots in the romantic nostalgia of chaos. One of the centres of this new wave is Glasgow School of Art, Scotland, where two of the four Cloth designers did their initial training.

The Cloth is a good example of that hybrid of art and design – the applied arts. The development of the applied arts in Britain has been like the flourishing of a wild, neglected corner of a park: undisturbed by the landscape gardener's ideas about formal composition, all kinds of strange plants may flourish, including those which would otherwise be rejected as weeds. The arts and crafts movement in Britain keeps resurfacing partly because several intellectuals in Britain go on trying to turn Britain back to the politics and aesthetic morality of John Ruskin and the aesthetic socialism of William Morris – both 19th-century thinkers of limited political relevance to the late twentieth century. Both thinkers were at heart anti-capitalist and in Britain (unlike Western Europe) the applied arts movement has generally been left rather than right in politics. This has encouraged the misfits in the design and art world to see the applied arts – the crafts – as a way of both doing their own thing and holding on to their values. The small independent designer-maker of textiles, furniture and pots only has to satisfy a very small range of clients; he or she is under none of the client or marketing pressure that constrain the industrial designer or the graphics or packaging designer. The ceramicists, metalsmiths and textile artists thus went off and did their own thing, unregarded and unsupported except in the art schools. In the early 1970s it was apparent to a few individuals that the applied arts might be an important asset so the Crafts Council was set up to support them.

Textiles, ceramics and furniture have been particularly interesting although that applied art of applied arts – jewellery – has undoubtedly been the most controversial. Unfortunately very few people see its relevance to design which is a pity because it has meant that dozens of decorative ideas and a lot of styling ability has gone unused in the wider product design/consumer market.

Ceramics, for example, is an odd phenomenon at this stage of the twentieth century. No one needs handmade pots to eat or drink from; contemporary pottery's function would seem to be entirely aesthetic, decorative and metaphorical. To that extent ceramics might be seen in the same light as contemporary painting and sculpture – useless, museum or gallery orientated, and searching for a role. More and more ceramicists are giving their work a content or turning their applied art into a commentary. This is inevitable. If a form or an activity no longer has a particular function then the artist or craftsman is free to follow his or her fancy. For example, Richard Slee's work (see page 24) is full of commentary: he is interested in the industrially produced decorative art of the English 19th century and also in the period between the two world wars when the suburbs in Britain grew rapidly and the homes were filled with peculiar sentimental knick-knacks. Both interests are made use of in Slee's work. A lot of ceramics in Britain is deliberately, demonstrably gestural as a way of slapping the factory and industrially designed product around the face. To that extent it is part of a continuum with fine art.

The exciting aspect about western design generally is that no one knows where it is all leading. What is predictable is that there will be a greater willingness on the part of younger designers to mix design or whatever they are doing with fine or applied arts. Industrial design proper – or as proper as it has become respectable to regard it – pretty square boxes in pastel shades or white and grey – has simply ran out of ideas. The simple desire for change as well as economic necessity is leading stylists out into different kinds of imagery. Whether this is a flash in the pan or the beginnings of a movement remains to be seen. If it does turn out to be just a flash in the pan it has nonetheless been, and continues to be, a very interesting one. Naturally we hope it is something more.

In particular it is the mix of references, images and new ideas which characterises a lot of contemporary British design. Amid glances towards Japan, Las Vegas, the Wiener Werkstatte, and medieval England there is a determination to make objects that have a *voice*, furniture or product design or fashion which provides entertainment, or solace, or both. Having started the industrial revolution, the British seem also to be among the first to seek ways of subverting the uniformity of the industrial age in its decline.

Peter Dormer

DIRECTORY

Directory of Designers
(Based on information supplied to
the Editor by the individual/s
concerned.)

Jenny Amon
(Ceramics)
c/o Royal College of Art
Kensington Gore
London SW7
01-584 5020

Atlantic Design
Ros Appleby, Felix Scarlett
(Product design)
6 Newburgh Street
London W1V 1LH
01-434 3328
*Product design – consumer, sports
equipment, marine equipment*

Ron Arad
(Design and art)
One-off Ltd
56 Neal Street
London WC2
01-379 7796
*Design and art, soft and hard, new and
old, accidental and intentional.*

Matthew Archer
(Product design)
Trading as:
Pirate Design
109a Chiswick High Road
Chiswick
London W4
01-994 6555

Paul Edward Atkinson
(Furniture, lighting, product design)
Trading as:
Atkinson Design Associates Ltd
12 Abbey Gate
Leicester LE4 1AB
0533 29494
*Office seating programme and desking;
low energy lighting programme and
range of shower units; product
diversification programme; various
restaurants, corporate interiors.*

Remo Avella
(Textiles, illustration)
46 Lots Road
Chelsea
London SW10 0QH
01-352 6723
*Printed display boards for Courtaulds,
book cover illustration for Heinemann.*

Fred Baier
(Design consultant)
79 Bartholomew Road
London NW5 2AH
01-267 2568
*Design consultancy work in furniture,
plus prototyping and manufacturing
'one-offs' including upholstered chairs
with specially designed woven fabrics.*

Douglas Barber
(Industrial Design)
14 Beverley Road
Colchester
Essex CO3 3NG

Chris Barlow
(Industrial design)
20 Pembridge Crescent
Bayswater
London W11 3DS
01-243 1718

Phil Baynes
(Graphic design)
c/o Royal College of Art
Kensington Gore
London SW7
01-584 5020

Alex Beleschenko
(Architectural stained glass)
6 Park Road
Polsloe Park
Exeter EX1 2HP
0392 213875
Represented by:
Public Arts Development Trust
City Gallery Arts Trust
Crafts Council
Andrew Moor Associates
*Architectural stained glass – leaded and
glass laminate; The Leicester Royal
Infirmary – interior stained glass screen;
Arup Associates – windows for a park
development.*

Tom E Binns
(Jewellery)
43 Beak Street
London W1
01-437 8291
*Jewellery, accessorising fashion in
London, Paris and New York;
advertising; film.*

Judy Blame
(Accessory design, styling, promotion)
Trading as:
Judy Blame & Fred Poodle
The House of Beauty and Culture
34-36 Stamford Road
London N1
01-254 7794
Represented by:
Mark Lebon (see entry)

David Blamey
(Painting, illustration)
9b Adelaide Grove
London W12
*The Billionth Press – founder of limited
edition artists' books.
Liberty prints, Elle magazine,
Departures magazine and Timney
Fowler prints*

Paul Burgess
(Textiles, illustration)
73 Pascoe Road
Hither Green
London
01-852 1600
*Printed display boards for Courtaulds;
print collections for Ritva Kariniemi at
'Extravert'; print collections for
'Extetique' by Amescote Ltd*

Karen Caldicott
(Illustration)
39 St Augustines Road
London NW1
01-485 2756/01-278 0290
*In 1985 formed R K Construction,
incorporating the design of clothes,
painted and printed fabrics. Thumb
Gallery Exhibition 1986. Bath
Contemporary Arts Fair 86*

The Cloth:
Fraser Taylor, Brian Bolger,
David Band, Helen Manning
*(Textiles, fashion, graphic design,
corporate identity).*
Trading as:
The Cloth
27-29 Union Street
London SE1
01-378 7738

Nigel Coates
(Architect)
Trading as:
Branson Coates Architects
61 Cambridge Street
London SW1V 4PS
01-821 8006/01-821 8246
Represented by:
Anne Brooks
Architecture; interiors; furniture; art and
theory of architecture as teacher, artist
and NATO member. He intends to
launch his own furniture and design
collection in Japan. Recent work
includes Metropole Restaurant Tokyo,
conversion and furniture; Silver
Jeweller's London; Jasper Conran's
house, London NW1; Jasper Conran's
shop, London SW7; Takeo Kikuchi's
shop and Jazz Room, Tokyo. Exhibitions:
ArkAlbion, Venice Guggenheim
(NATO); D'uomo Forum, Middelburg;
Gamma City, Air Gallery, London
(NATO); Chair Exhibitions, Shiseido
Gallery, Tokyo.

David Cole
(Industrial design)
7a Coolsara Park
Lisburn
Co Antrim
Northern Ireland CT28 3BG
Cole is currently working for Motor
Panels, Coventry.

Calum Colvin
(Photography)
December 10 Studios
B2 Roadside
Metropolitan Wharf
Wapping Wall
London E1 1AA
01-481 3506
Mostly 'fine art' photography, large scale
colour work, occasional commercial
work, product photography.

Jacqueline Cowper
(Jewellery)
151 Highgate Road
Parliament Hill
London NW5
01-485 9326
Represented by:
Monolith, London
Has completed 2 collections of jewellery
in collaboration with Keith Spicer
(menswear designer, buyer and fashion
director for Bazaar Shops). Working on
collection of jewellery for NEXT shops.

Jane Dillon
(Consultant industrial design)
2nd floor
Telescope House
63 Farringdon Road
London EC1
01-831 6536
Specialist in furniture and lighting.
Completed two wardrobes for the
Vienna British Design exhibition, 1986.
Range of office chairs for Casas,
Barcelona.

Tom Dixon
(Furniture design)
30 All Saints Road
London W11
01-727 0134
Manufactures a range of new and old
metals in a 'reaction against
minimalism as a return to decoration'.
Aquariums, seating, chandeliers and
table for Kings Road Tea
Rooms/Chocolate Shop; column capitols
and chandelier for Metropole
Restaurant, Tokyo.

Dirk van Dooren
(Multi-disciplinary design)
17 Rainbow Street
London SE5
01-708 4535
Lambeth Video; I.M.A.G.I.N.E.
consultant; London Sinfonietta;
part-time lecturer at Harrow College
of Art.

Andre M C Dubreuil
(Interior design and architecture)
12 Bassett Road
London W10
01-968 9468
Represented by:
Themes and Variations
231 Westbourne Grove
London W11
Refurbishing a bar-restaurant and an
18th century house in the country.
Furniture, lighting, painting, interior
design, everything to do with houses.

James Dyson
(Product origination, product design)
Trading as:
Prototypes Ltd
Sycamore House
Bathford
Bath
Avon BA1 7RS
0225 858713/Fax: 0225 852495
Recent projects have included: 'G Force'
cyclonic vacuum cleaner; electric
wheelchair for Chairpower Ltd;
amphibious vehicle for Rotork Ltd;
'Ballbarrow' wheelbarrow; domestic
appliances.

John England
(Illustration)
c/o Royal College of Art
Illustration Department
Exhibition Road
South Kensington
London SW7
01-584 5020
His work 'offers a future. Stuffy
"designers", young and old, always
playing down their work, scared of
clients not accepting them, will never
satisfy me. I have no apprehension
about using the latest technology, the
obvious solution to the new'. "Another
World Design" thrives on the idea of a
new gravity that pulls people towards it
out of the lure of 'History' – it will bend
and break 'The Rule' for the future.'

Georgina von Etzdorf
(Textile design)
The Avenue
Odstock
Wiltshire SP5 4JA
(0722) 26625

Fric and Frack
(Furniture and lighting design)
Unit C9
Metropolitan Workshops
Enfield Road
London N1
01-241 5118
Represented by:
Alan McDonald and Fritz Soloman
Produce a range of domestic
lighting/furniture, using found objects.

John Galliano
(Fashion design)
27-31 Macklin Street
London WC2
01-405 5598
Represented by:
Jean Bennett

Georgina Godley
(Fashion design)
30 All Saints Road
London W11
01-727 0134
Collections, including 'Body and Soul,
Summer 1986' Lump and Bump, Winter
1986 in Browns and Bloomingdales.

Daniel Grey
The Grey Organisation
(Multi-disciplinary, multi-media design)
13 Bruce Road
London E3
01-980 8144
Multi-media, furniture, painting,
fashion, event. Worked with Christopher
Hobbs, among others, on Derek
Jarman's 'Caravaggio'.

Oriel Harwood
(Architectural ceramics)
c/o Bentley Hall
Bentley
Ipswich
Suffolk
0473 311435
Work is press moulded and handbuilt in
earthenware, then coloured using slips
underglaze, colours transparent and
metallic glaze, enamels and lustres.
Aims to build a total environment with
ceramic architectural details, from
curtain poles to fireplace.

Maura Heslop
(Jewellery)
35 St Lukes Avenue
Clapham
London SW4
01-627 3928
Exhibitions at Saunders Design Gallery
– August 1985, Adam Gallery 1986.
Retail outlets include Detail, Colin Swift
and Monolith, London.

David Hiscock
(Photography, graphic design)
December 10 Studios
B2 Roadside
Metropolitan Wharf
Wapping Wall
London E1 1AA
01-481 3506
Photography – fashion, portraiture, still-life, record jackets. Photography with additive/subtractive elements (drawing, painting, scratching, sanding). Royal Photographic Society – Bath 1987.

Geoff Hollington
(Industrial design)
Trading as:
Hollington Associates
The Old Schoolhouse
68a Leonard Street
London EC2A 4QX
01-739 3501
Industrial design, particularly high volume office furniture and systems and consumer products. Chess playing computers for CXG, Hong Kong; 'Basys' office chair for Syba Ltd, UK; three major projects in progress for Herman Miller Inc, USA.

Nicole Hood
(Ceramics)
11 Myrdle Court
Myrdle Street
London E1 1HP
01-377 1970
Hand painting on factory-produced plates for 'Kunst', London. Plans to expand into teapots, cups, etc.

Jim Horrobin
(Blacksmith/design)
The Forge
Carhampton
Minehead
Somerset TA24 6NL
0643 821293
Represented by:
Aspects Gallery, London Crafts Council

Paul Huxley
(Artist)
29 St Albans Avenue
London W4 5LL
01-431 1031
Represented by:
Juda Rowan Gallery
11 Tottenham Mews
London W1P 9PJ

Simon Josebury
(Illustration and painting)
11 St Annes Flats
Doric Way
London NW1 1LG
01-387 5131
Illustration and painting. Commissions include 'The Wire' and 'Elle' magazines.

Lindsey Keir
(Textile Design)
c/o Royal College of Art
Kensington Gore
London SW7
01-584 5020

Daniel Lane
(Glass)
Glassworks
56-60 Metropolitan Works
Enfield Road
London N1
01-254 9096
Represented by:
One Off Ltd

Mark Lebon
(Photography, film, communications design)
E/20 New Cavendish Street
London W1
01-486 9065/01-939 0888/
01-402 0144
Represented by:
Ray Petri
Photography – fashion, portraits for Tatler, I-D; publishing – co-founder/ editor of 'The Fred'; founder of 'Reely Film Club' integrating music and film; representing artists – Boy George initially, Chris Nemeth and Judy Blame.

Mary Little
(Interior design)
37 Henty Close
London SW11 4AH
01-585 1100

Marion McDonald
(Ceramics)
27 Union Street
London SE1
01-407 0009

Andrew McRae
(Design education)
c/o National Art School
PO Box 5098
Boroko
Papua New Guinea
McRae is currently teaching design in Papua New Guinea.

Tom Mitchell
(Environmental research)
5 South Street
Reading
Berks RG1 4QP
0734 508368
Writing and research on 'perceptually based design' (at the University of Reading, England). Mitchell is trying to evaluate environments, (to date, by varying spatial scale and musical tempo) to see how changes affect people psychologically or perceptually. This work is related to new concepts of 'the environment', touching on ambient music, video, light intensity, colour and image complexity as well as combinations of these factors.

Gary Morga
(Design)
Trading as:
Gary Morga Design
17 Kew Terrace
Glasgow G12 0TE
041 335 5274
Represented by:
Michael Policella
5815 Williamson
Dearborn
Michigan 48126
USA
Lighting product design, metal furniture design. Extending the Luminum lighting system range.

John Moore
(Shoe Design)
The House of Beauty and Culture
36-36 Stamford Road
London N1
01-254 7794

Jasper Morrison
(Furniture, interior design)
85 Oxford Gardens
London W10 5UL
01-968 3624/01-722 3612

NATO: Catrins Beevor, Martin Bension Nigel Coates, Peter Fleissig, Robert Mull, Christina Norton, Mark Prizeman, Melanie Sainsbury, Carlos Villanueva
(Architecture, Polemic)
Trading as:
NATO: Narrative Architecture Today
NATO Magazine, London
c/o The Architecture Association
34-36 Bedford Square
London WC1B 3ES
01-636 0974/01-821 8006/01-821 8246
Current work: architecture as 'an elastic organisation'; NATO's activity can vary from practice to product, from building to drawing, from vision to video, from marketplace to magazine – a pursuance of current lifestyle as the 'sustaining parallel to the design of cities'. Applications include Venice Bienalle 1985; NATO"s Gamma City, Air Gallery, London 1985 and on tour to Edinburgh and Bristol; and the Chair Exhibition in Tokyo in 1986.

Christopher Nemeth
(Fashion design)
The House of Beauty and Culture
34-36 Stamford Road
London N1
01-254 7794
Represented by:
Mark Lebon
One-offs with chosen quality fabrics for Bazaar, London; 'Kunst', Wardour Street, London; 'Postsack' collection which combines with Judy Blame's 'old rope' collection for 'House of Beauty and Culture', London.

Susan Nemeth
(Ceramics)
27 Union Street
London SE1
01-407 0009/01-250 2196
Press moulded and slab built porcelain ceramics, highly decorated with oxides and body stains. Outlets include Liberty's 'One-off' department, London, The Design Centre, London, St James Gallery, Bath, Peter Dingley Gallery, Tetbury and Luten Clarey Stern Inc, New York. Also pottery tutor for mentally handicapped adults, Streatham and Tooting Institute, London.

Rifat Ozbek
(Fashion design)
18 Haunch of Venison Yard
London W1
01-408 0625
The first Ozbek collection was shown in October 1984. Since then he has launched major collections twice yearly in London and sells in Europe and USA.

Cindy Palmano
(Photography)
39 Great Russell Street
Bloomsbury
London WC1
01-636 2343

Julian Powell-Tuck
David Connor
Gunnar Orefelt
(Architecture and design)
Trading as:
Powell-Tuck, Connor & Orefelt Ltd
10 Chelsea Wharf
15 Lots Road
London SW10
01-351 5877/8
Current work: Architecture, interior design, furniture, product design. New studio house, Battersea Church Road, London SW11; conversion of single family dwelling, London SW7; conversion of garage to design studio development, London W11; design for apartment development, Napa Creek Terrace, Napa, California and design for residential apartments, St George's Wharf, Pimlico.

Paul Priestman
(Design)
8 Hillside Mansions
Jacksons Lane
London N6 5SS
01-340 7513
Having developed the prototypes for a heating and radiator system while a student at the Royal College of Art, Priestman has recently launched a series of electrical radiators based on his original concept. He intends to develop more heating appliances which he argues are more pieces of furniture today than pure engineering.

John Richmond/Maria Cornejo
(Fashion design)
Trading as:
Richmond Cornejo
Represented by:
Marysia Woronieka
No 1 Chelsea Manor Studio
London SW3
01-351 7411
Work on three basic lines: manufacturing and producing in Italy under the name Richmond Cornejo; manufacturing and producing mainly knitwear range in Japan under the name 3-D Richmond Cornejo; range of menswear produced in the name of 3-D London. Retail outlets in the UK: Joseph, Jones, Bazaar and Warehouse, Glasgow.

Sheila Rock
(Photography)
Studio 20
Liddell Road
Maygrove Road
London NW6
01-624 7521
Portraiture and fashion; editorial; advertising; music business.

Esperanza Romero
(Architectural ceramics))
401½ Workshops
401½ Wandsworth Road
London SW8
01-622 7621/01-727 4764

Vonnie Roudette
(Artist, interior design)
13 Holly House
Hawthorn Walk
London W10
01-960 6296
Current work includes drawing, painting and screen printed images on cloth and paper; applications in fashion, video, window display and design, carpets, interiors. Has completed window design and display for Issey Miyake's two London shops – involving use of pattern imagery on windows, backdrops and relating to stock in shop and interior. Work is using printed images on large sculptured garments and headdresses. Future plans include work in 3-D space such as theatre. About to embark on specific design projects with carpet manufacturers and also cloth retailers.

Seymour Powell
(Product Development)
2c Seagrove Road
London SW6
01-381 6433

Random
Ian Dampney
(Industrial design)
326 Kensal Road
London W10 5BZ
01-969 7702
Current work is on the development of mechanical/electro-mechanical products with electronics packaging through all prototype and test rig stages to preproduction runs and production drawing and liaison. Recent projects include the Synthaxe – guitar synthesiser input; industrial respirator for dust/fume laden environments; recording/broadcasting studio mixing desk; portable chiropodist/ physiotherapist operating chair. Plans in the long term: centring entire projects on one computer system from early prototype to production, including electronics layout.

Tim Shaw
(Glass design)
14 Paddock Gardens
Crystal Palace
London SE19
01-670 9614
Predominantly hand-blown glass. Producing vase or urn-related forms (non-functional) as 'one-off' pieces or limited editions of similar pieces.

Richard Slee
(Ceramics)
12a Upper Hamilton Road
Brighton BN1 5DF
0273 501946
Represented by:
Aspects Gallery
3 Whitfield Street
London W1

TAG Design Partnership
Tony Wills/Greg Holme
(Product, industrial and interior design)
39-41 North Road
Islington
London N7 9DP
01-607 9374
Furniture and lighting design for mass production and for architectural/interior design projects. Prototypes and modelmaking and one-offs. Futon Company, new furniture range, Harrods Way In, shopfitting and display items; Lloyds building, design of screens; IBM Basingstoke, special lighting; Wang European Headquarters, special lighting.

Richard Torry
(Fashion design)
Trading as:
Richard Torry (London) Ltd
2nd floor
57 Old Compton Street
London W1
01-439 3656
Represented in Japan by:
Vivid/Hanae Mori
5th floor
London Station Department
Shin-Ooju Building
2-1-8 Ookubo
Shinjuku - ku
Tokyo
010 81 03 2070061
Shop in Isetan Department Store, Tokyo, finance by Vivid/Hanae Mori; wallpaper and mannequins also designed by Torry.

Lisa Vandy
(Metalwork and Jewellery)
12 Greenland Street
London NW1
01-485 3593
Represented by:
Marysia Woronieka (Jewellery)
01-351 7411
Alison Hargreaves (Clocks and mirrors)
01-405 5598
Sheet metal work – clocks and mirrors, fashion jewellery.

Sasha Ward
(Glass maker/designer)
171 Mayenne Place
Devizes
Wilts
0380 77507

David Watkins
*(Jeweller, visiting professor at
Royal College of Art)*
Crafts Council
12 Waterloo Place
London SW1
01-930 4811
*During the past two years Watkins has
concentrated on making large sculpture
in metal. Recent work in jewellery has
been devoted to neckpiece elements.
Their imagery responds to a variety of
experiences, including visits to the Far
East and Australia.*

Daniel Weil
(Industrial design)
Trading as:
Parenthesis Ltd
and
Gerard Taylor and Daniel Weil
3 Plough Yard
London EC2A 3LP
01-247 5628
*Industrial design, interior retail and
corporate design, product research and
development. Weil and his partner
Gerard Taylor have set up a design
consultancy whose clients include
ESPRIT, Tube Investments and The
National Coal Board.*

Kirsten Woodward
(Hat design)
Trading as:
Kirsten Woodward Hats
Unit 26
Portobello Green Arcade
281 Portobello Road
London W10
01-960 0090
*Collection each season. Hats from Karl
Lagerfeld at Lagerfeld; commission
work for Chanel and Fendi; hats for
video and advertising; Winter 1986/7
collection based on Mad Max films;
Ascot hats (miniature) in black and
white; hats like coiffures in leather or
organza.*

**Wire Up and Finish Painting
Iain Irving/Judith Findlay**
(Design, art, installations)
10 Canongate Venture
New Street
Edinburgh EH8 8BN
*Lighting, furniture, installations,
artwork, art books and writing. Using
carefully chosen, discarded objects for
new uses. Construction using metal,
wood and glass – involving welding,
painting and writing.*

Tom Dixon, chairs

DIRECTORY

LONDON

Adam, 62 Walcot Square, SE11
(01 582 1260)
Air Gallery,
6 Rosebery Avenue, EC1
(01 278 7751)
Albion Contemporary Arts,
Metropolitan Wharf,
Wapping Wall, E1
(01 481 4259)
Anatol Orient, Portobello Rd, W10
Anderson O'Day,
5 St Quintin Avenue, W10
(01 969 8085)
Angela Flowers Gallery,
11 Tottenham Mews W1
(01 637 3089)
Anne Berthold,
1 Langley Court, WC2
(01 836 7357)
Anthony D'Offay,
9 & 23 Dering Street, W1
(01 629 1578/01 499 4695)
Argenta, 82 Fulham Road, SW3
(01 584 3119)
Artefact, 37 Windmill Street, W1
(01 580 9684)
Art for Offices,
O & N Wreho, Metropolitan Wharf,
Wapping Wall, E1
(01 481 1337)
Art Show, 23 Jerdan Place SW6
(01 385 5207)
Art Space, 84 St Peters Street, N1
(01 359 7002)
Aspects,
by appointment with Sharon Plant
(01 354 3073)
Association of Illustrators Gallery,
1 Colville Place, W1
(01 636 4100)
Barbican Centre,
Silk Street, Barbican, EC2
(01 638 4141)
Battersea Arts Centre,
176 Lavender Hill, SW11
(01 223 6557)
Boilerhouse
Victoria & Albert Museum,
Cromwell Road
Exhibition Rd SW7
(01 581 5273)
British Crafts Centre,
43 Earlham Street, WC2
(01 836 6993)
Camden Arts Centre,
Arkwright Road, NW3
(01 435 2643)

Casson Gallery,
73 Marylebone High Street, W1
(01 487 5080)
Centre 181 Gallery,
181 King Street, W1
(01 741 3696)
Chenil Art Gallery,
183 Kings Road, SW3
(01 352 8581)
Co-Existence,
2 Conduit Buildings, Floral St, WC2
(01 240 2746)
Colin Swift,
48 Monmouth Street, WC2
(01 836 8865)
Contemporary Art Society,
20 John Islip Street, SW1
(01 821 5323)
Crafts Council,
8 Waterloo Place, SW1
(01 930 4811)
Craft Shop,
Victoria & Albert Museum
Cromwell Road, SW7
(01 589 5070)
Crucial,
204 Kensington Park Road, W11
(01 229 1940)
Cylinder Gallery,
39 Great Russell Street, WC1
(01 251 2334)
Design Council,
*Design Centre and
Design Magazine*,
28 Haymarket, SW1
(01 839 8000)
Detail *(jewellery)*,
49 Endell Street, WC2
(01 379 6940)
7 Dials,
52 Earlham Street, WC2
(01 240 5470)
Diorama
Arts Centre,
14 Peto Place, NW1
(01 487 5598)
Dryden Street Gallery,
5 Dryden Street, WC2
Edward Totah Gallery,
39 Floral Street, WC2
(01 379 6341)
Electrum *(jewellery)*,
21 South Molton Street, W1
(01 629 6325)
Francis Kyle,
9 Maddox Street, W1
(01 499 6870)
Gallery 44,
309a New Kings Road, SW6
(01 736 6887)

Glasshouse,
65 Longacre, WC2
(01 836 9785)
Graeme Dowling Contemporary Art,
6 Shillingford Street, N1
(01 359 6106)
Graffiti,
27 Bruton Place, W1
(01 486 7647)
ICA,
The Mall, SW1
(01 930 0493)
Jonathan Pook,
915 Fulham Road, SW6
(01 736 1404)
Joseph pour la Maison,
16 Sloane Street, SW1
Kodak Photographic Gallery,
180 High Holborn, WC1
(01 405 7841)
Liberty & Co,
Regent Street, W1
(01 734 1234)
Lisson Gallery,
66-68 Bell Street, NW1
(01 262 1539)
3-D Gallery,
Metropolitan Wharf, Wapping Wall, E1
Monolith,
6 Upper James Street
(01 437 2310)
Nicholas Treadwell,
36 Chiltern Street, W1
(01 486 1414)
Nicola Jacobs,
9 Cork Street, W1
(01 437 3868)
Nigel Greenwood Gallery,
4 New Burlington Street, W1
(01 434 3795)
One Off,
56 Neal Street, WC2
(01 379 7796)
Paton Gallery, 2 Langley Court, WC2
(01 379 7854)
Photographers Gallery,
5 & 8 Great Newport Street, WC2
(01 240 5511/2)
Portobello Green Workshops,
Portobello Road
(under the Westway flyover)
Riverside Studios,
Crisp Road, W6
(01 741 2251)
Submarine Gallery,
294 Pentonville Road, N1 9NR
(01 837 2045)
Themes and Variations,
231 Westbourne Grove, W1
(01 727 5531)

Waddington Galleries,
Cork Street, W1
(01 439 1866)
Whitechapel Art Gallery,
Whitechapel High Street, E1
(01 377 0107)

BRIGHTON

Birmingham Arts Lab,
Holt Street, Birmingham B7 4BA
(021 359 4192)
Holt Street Gallery,
Unit of Aston Centre for Arts,
Gosta Green, Birmingham B4 7ET
(021 359 3979)
Ikon Gallery,
58-72 John Bright Street,
Birmingham B1 1PN
(021 643 0708)
Midlands Art Centre,
Foyle House, Cannon Hill Park,
Birmingham B12
(021 440 4221)
Timaeus,
2a Salisbury Road,
Moseley B13 8JS
(021 449 7301)

BIRMINGHAM

Axis,
12 Market Street, The Lanes,
Brighton, Sussex
(0273 203193)
Brighton Polytechnic Gallery,
Faculty of Art and Design,
Brighton Polytechnic,
Grand Parade, Brighton
Gardner Centre Gallery,
University of Sussex,
Falmer, Brighton,
East Sussex BN1 9RA
(0273 685447)

BRENTFORD

Brentford Watermans,
40 High Street, Brentford,
Middlesex TW8 0DS
(01 586 3312/1176)

BRISTOL

Arnolfini,
16 Narrow Quay,
Bristol BS1 4QA
(0272 299191)
Bristol Arts Centre,
4-5 Kings Square,
Bristol 2
(0272 45008)
Equation *(fashion),*
15-19 Queens Road,
Clifton,
Bristol BS8 1HP
(0272 211394)
Watershed, Carons Road, Bristol
(0272 276444)

EXETER

Spacex Gallery,
45 Preston Street, Exeter,
Devon
(0392 31786)

HULL

Ferens Art Gallery,
Queen Victoria Square,
Hull (0482 222750)

LEEDS

City Art Gallery,
The Headrow, Leeds
(0532 462495)
Leeds Polytechnic Gallery,
H Block, Leeds Polytechnic,
Calverley Street, Leeds 1
(0532 31751)
St Pauls Gallery,
5 Bishopsgate Street,
Leeds (0532 456421)
University Gallery Leeds,
Department of Fine Art,
University of Leeds L52 9JT
(0532 31751)

LIVERPOOL

Bluecoat Gallery,
School Lane, Liverpool L1 3BX
(051 709 5689)
Open Eye Gallery,
90-92 Whitechapel,
Liverpool L3 8EL
(051 709 9460)
Walker Art Gallery,
William Brown Street,
Liverpool L3
(051 227 5234)

MANCHESTER

City Art Gallery,
Mosley Street,
Manchester M2 3JL
(061 236 9422)
Gallery of Modern Art *(Athenaeum),*
Princess Street, Manchester
(061 236 9422)
Colin Jellicoe Gallery,
82 Portland Street, Manchester
(061 236 2716)
Whitworth Art Gallery,
University of Manchester,
Whitworth Park,
Manchester M15 6ER
(061 273 4865)

NEWCASTLE-UPON-TYNE

Carouste Gulbenkian Gallery,
Peoples Theatre Arts Group,
Stephenson Road,
Newcastle-upon-Tyne NE5 5QF
(0632 655020)
Laing Art Gallery,
Higham Place,
Newcastle-upon-Tyne NE1 8AG
(0632 26989/27734)
Side Gallery
(photography),
9 Side, Newcastle-upon-Tyne
(0632 22208)

NOTTINGHAM

Focus Gallery,
108 Derby Road, Nottingham
(0602 417913)
Midland Group Gallery,
24-32 Carlton Street,
Nottingham NG1 1NN
(0602 592636)

OXFORD

Museum of Modern Art,
30 Pembroke Street, Oxford
(0865 722733)

PLYMOUTH

Plymouth Arts Centre,
38 Looe Street, Plymouth
(0752 60060)

PORTSMOUTH

Aspex Gallery,
27 Brougham Road, Portsmouth,
(0705 812121)

SCOTLAND

ABERDEEN

Artspace,
21 Castle Street, Aberdeen
(0224 50126)

EDINBURGH

Fruitmarket,
29 Market Street, Edinburgh
(031 226 5781)
Graeme Murray Gallery,
2 Eyre Crescent, Edinburgh
(031 556 8689)
New 57 Gallery,
29 Market Street,
Edinburgh EH1 1DF
(031 225 2383)
Richard Demarco Gallery,
10 Jeffrey Street, Edinburgh
(031 557 0707)

GLASGOW

Compass Gallery,
178 West Regent Street, Glasgow
(041 221 6370)
Third Eye Centre,
350 Sauchiehall Street, Glasgow G2
(041 332 7521)

WALES

CARDIFF

Chapter Gallery,
*Chapter Workshops and
Centre for the Arts,*
Market Road, Canton, Cardiff CF6
(0222 396061)
Oriel,
53 Charles Street, Cardiff CF1 4EH
(0222 395548/395549)

NORTHERN IRELAND

BELFAST

Arts Council Gallery,
Bedford House, Bedford Street,
Belfast 2 (0232 221402)
Bell Gallery,
2 Malone Road, Belfast BT9 5BN
(0232 662998)
Octagon Gallery,
1 Lower Crescent, Belfast BT7 1RN
(0232 46259)

NEW YORK

Alternative Museum,
17 White Street, NYC
(966 4444)
Area X,
200 E 10th Street
(477 1177)
Art & Industrie,
594 Broadway,
(431 1661)
Artists Space,
223 West Broadway,
NY 10013
Attitude Art,
184 Franking Street
(Hudson & Greenwich)
NYC 10013 (966 1322)
Avenue B,
167 Avenue B (473 4600)
Bockley Gallery,
59 E 7th Street
(420 9835)
Cash Newhouse,
170 Avenue B
(473 4600)
Ceres Gallery,
91 Franklin Street, NYC
Chronocide Galleries,
155 Avenue B (10th Street),
NYC 10009 (460 8101)
Civilian Warfare,
614 E 9th Street,
NYC 10011 (475 7498)
Civilisation,
Second Avenue E 4th
Clodagh Ross and Williams
(furniture shop)
122 St Marks Place,
NYC (505 1774)
Dash and Dash,
632 E 11th *(Between B & C)*
(475 7406)
Detail,
Spring Street,
NY 10012
Diane Brown,
100 Greene Street
(219 1060)
Eastman Wahmendorf Gallery,
216 E 10th Street
(420 9109)

Emily Harvey Gallery,
537 Broadway, 2nd Floor
(925 7651)
Freddy the Dreamer,
40 Rivington, NYC
Holly Soloman Gallery,
724 5th Avenue
(757 7777)
Iguana International Art,
59 Stanton at Eldridge
(982 4358)
International with Monument,
111 E 7th Street
(420 0517)
J N Herlin Inc,
68 Thompson Street
(431 8732)
Jim Diaz Gallery,
223 E 10th Street
(420 9174)
J Walter Thompson Exhibition Space,
466 Lexington Avenue, NYC
Limbo,
647 E 9th Street,
NYC (228 3000)
La Galleria Seconde Class,
6 E 1st Street,
NYC 10003 (260 4019)
M-13,
440 E 9th Street, NYC
9th Precinct Gallery,
309 E 5th Street, NYC
Painting Space,
122-150 1st Avenue, NYC
Paula Cooper,
155 Wooster Street, NYC
Phoenix City,
184 E 6th Street
(982 1246)
Pictogram,
443 E 9th Street
(865 5476)
Pompeii,
210 Forsyth NYC 10002
(260 7747)
Postmasters Gallery,
66 Avenue A
(477 5630)
PPOW, 216,
E 10th Street
(447 4084)
Segal,
568 Broadway, NYC
(431 0010)
Semaphore,
462 West Broadway, NYC 10012
(228 7990)
Semaphore East,
157 Avenue B at 110th Street,
NYC 10009 (475 2130)
Sharpe Gallery,
175 Avenue B, NYC
(777 4622)
Sperone Westwater,
142 Greene Street,
NY 10012
St Marks Gallery,
411 E 9th Street
(505 9716)

Storefront
for Art and Architecture,
(corner Lafayette
and Kenmare Streets, NYC)
Terra Artis Gallery,
61 E 3rd Street,
NYC 10009 (874 0088)
Thaw Malin Gallery,
530 E 13th Street,
NYC (475 1350)
The 5 and Dime,
208 E 7th Street
(858 9346)
303 Gallery,
303 Park Avenue South
(477 4917)
Visual Arts Gallery,
137 Wooster Street, NYC
Visual Arts Museum,
209 E 23rd Street,
NYC 10010 (679 7350)
White Columns,
325 Sprint Street
(between Washington and Greenwich),
NYC 10013 (924 4212)
Zeus Trabia, 437 E 9th Street,
(505 6330)